THE MIDDLE EAST—AND WHY

THE MIDDLE EAST
—AND WHY

CLARKE NEWLON

DODD, MEAD & COMPANY

NEW YORK

956
New

1 2 3 4 5 6 7 8 9 10

Library of Congress Cataloging in Publication Data

Newlon, Clarke.
    The Middle East—and why.

    Bibliography: p.
    Includes index.
    SUMMARY: Discusses the importance of the Middle
East throughout history with emphasis on the factors—
oil, politics, and money—which make it important in
the world today.
    1. Near East—Juvenile literature. [1. Near East]
I. Title.
DS44.N48   956   76-53443
ISBN 0-396-07425-1

Contents

CHAPTER I

The Critical Land

It was October 17, 1973. The four men in dark business suits who arrived in a limousine at the east gate of the White House and were admitted virtually unnoticed were as anonymous as four shadows.

Through the very security-minded entrance hall and down the corridor, the four were escorted to the Oval Office where they were ushered in without waiting. There they found President Richard Nixon, Secretary of State Henry Kissinger, and Under Secretary Joseph Sisco, State's number one Middle East expert.

The leader of the four visitors was Omar Saqqaf, then Foreign Minister of Saudi Arabia, the world's largest oil-producing nation. Two of his colleagues and fellow Foreign Ministers were Sheikh Sabah al-Ahmad al-Jabar al-Sabah of Kuwait and Abdelaziz Bouteflika of Algeria. Together these three nations represented a supply of billions of barrels of oil on which the United States was infinitely dependent. The fourth man was Ahmed Taibi Benhima, Foreign Minister of Morocco, not a member of OPEC but influential in Middle East politics.

The seven men talked of the war which was building up to full fury between Egypt and Israel. The ministers may have presented a peace program (as they later told a skeptical *New York Times*, the only newspaper to get wind of the meeting). Most importantly, Saudi Arabia's Omar Saqqaf presented the President with a letter from his ruling monarch, King Faisal of the House of Sa'ud, which warned in uncharacteristically blunt language that if the United States did not stop supplying Israel with arms and other military supplies within forty-eight hours the result would be an oil embargo. It was at least the second such direct warning.

President Nixon listened and explained to Saqqaf that the policy of the United States in that regard had been firmly set; there was no possibility, he regretted, of meeting King Faisal's request.

The top officers of the top oil conglomerates had made desperate efforts to warn the Nixon regime that King Faisal was solidly inflexible in the intent behind his warning, but the President's sources—State, Defense, and the CIA—had assured him that the Arab threat was all bluff and would never be carried out. Oil, they said, had to have a market. Today, neither the White House nor State will admit the circumstances of the Faisal letter.

The foreign ministers left the White House. They had gone in temperish, because they had tried to see Mr. Nixon the day before and been refused. Their mood as they flew back to their home capitals was not kindly.

Two days after the meeting, on October 19, Nixon asked Congress to vote an additional $2.2 billion for aid to Israel.

The day following, October 20, the Saudi Arabians

gave their reply: a complete embargo on all oil shipments to the United States. The embargo was accompanied with production cutbacks from Saudi Arabia and other Middle East countries, which would have the result of starving the United States, and probably other countries, of oil.

The chaos that resulted came almost immediately, especially in the United States. Congress empowered the President to allocate petroleum products throughout the country, section by section, to avoid discrimination. Service stations, their supplies reduced by curtailments from the producers, worked out their own rationing systems, usually by closing part of the day or the week. Long lines formed at the gasoline pumps. Motorists cancelled trips, speed limits on the highways were cut to fifty-five miles an hour and actually enforced for a time. There was talk of unheated homes in New England and other colder areas of the country, of freezing families. Thermostats in homes and offices were turned down from the seventies to sixty-eight to save fuel, and home lights were turned off to save energy generally. The Pentagon worried about having or getting sufficient fuel for ships and planes and its highly mechanized land forces.

The price of gasoline, fuel oil, and other petroleum products shot up and up; the price of gasoline eventually doubled.

Being important in the affairs of the world is nothing unique to the Middle East, not at this late date. For hundreds of centuries the area has been singularly salient to

the rest of the world—geographically, historically, culturally. Here the continents of Europe, Asia, and Africa
come together to form a crossroads where the peoples of
the world have met to trade, quarrel, and exchange their
accumulated knowledge since man learned to reason and
communicate.

In Mesopotamia, now Iraq, nomad tribes established
the earliest beginnings of permanent settlements. That
was some ten or twelve thousand years ago, and from those
caves and mud huts along the Tigris and Euphrates rivers
evolved our present civilization. From the Middle East
came the first wheel, the first alphabet, the first number-
ing system, the first monotheistic religion, the worship of
one god; from here came the first concept of the supremacy of law instead of force in man's dealings with his
fellows.

Here in the Middle East were born three of the world's
great religions: Judaism, Christianity, and Islam, established in that order. Oddly, these divergent and sometimes
warring faiths all trace their origins back to the Old Testament records and to the same man—Abraham. Similar
versions of many of the same stories—Noah and the ark,
Jonah, and Samson—appear in both the Old Testament
and the Koran.

The term "Middle" East is credited to the American
Naval tactician and historian Captain Alfred Thayer
Mahan. Later it was perpetuated by the military in World
War II, though the composition of the area then and now
varies considerably, depending on the authority.

Certain countries virtually always are included: those

of the heartland—Lebanon, Syria, Israel, and Jordan; the neighboring nations of Turkey, Egypt, Iraq, and Iran; the entities of the Arabian Peninsula—Saudi Arabia, Qatar, Bahrain, Kuwait, the United Arab Emirates, Oman, the People's Democratic Republic of Yemen, the Yemen Arab Republic; and the Sudan.

Many geographers, particularly Arabs, also throw in the linking countries they call the "Maghreb" or "West," which lie to the west, but which we know as the North African nations of Libya, Tunisia, Algeria, and Morocco, plus the Spanish Sahara, also called Spanish North Africa.

All of the above are Arab by heritage and language except three—Turkey, Israel, and Iran.

Mahan thought of this hot, dry, and predominantly flat land as a hub; it is also a road to major waterways which both divide and link the continents of Africa, Asia, and Europe. The Middle East accommodates within its borders the Red Sea and the Persian Gulf, the Gulf of Aden and the Gulf of Oman. It is on—borders—the Indian Ocean and the Mediterranean, Arabian, and Black seas, and for hundreds of years it provided the most direct routes East to West, West to East, until the explorations of the fifteenth and sixteenth centuries opened a sea route to India. Later, in the nineteenth century, came the Suez Canal, linking the Red Sea and the Mediterranean.

The Middle East has an area of six million square miles and more, depending on which countries you include, and a population of from 150 to 200 million, using the same formula, although no really serious census has ever been taken. Whatever figure you take, add another thirty or

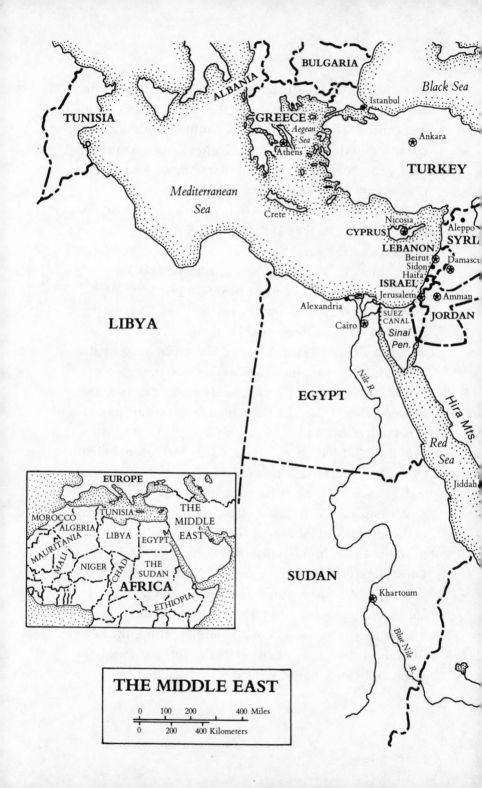

THE MIDDLE EAST

| 0 | 100 | 200 | | 400 Miles |

| 0 | 200 | 400 Kilometers |

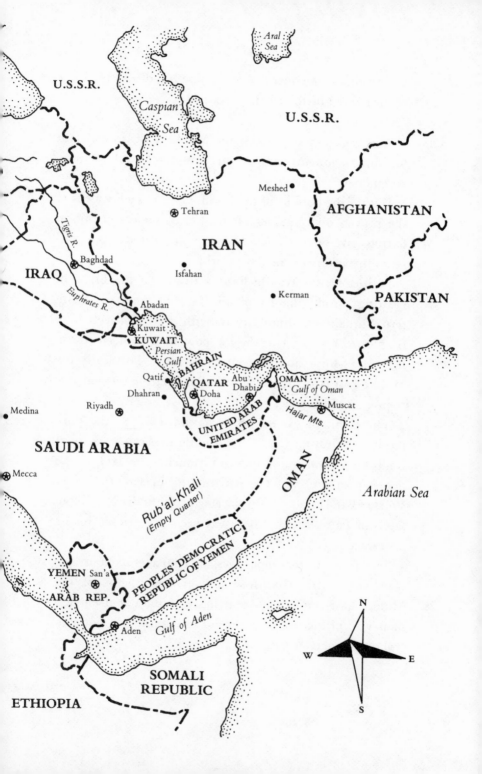

so million for the next ten years. The Middle East has one of the highest birth rates in the world.

And back to today: today the Middle East is important for three eminently important reasons—the oil, politics, and money.

Within the borders of the Middle East lies 60 percent of the proven oil resources of the world, some 450 billion barrels, give or take a few billion. And oil today is a matter of survival to the modern world.

Politically the Middle East is always on the brink of creating world calamity of one kind or another. Its internal squabbles, almost always with overt or covert help from one or another of the big powers, have been straining nerves for a quarter century or more. Politically the Middle East is an atomic blunderbuss waiting for someone to press the little black button.

The chain of events which have led up to the most recent political tangles of the Middle East can, except for traditional rivalries among governments, be laid at the doorstep of one act: the partitioning of Palestine after World War II and the displacement of hundreds of thousands of Palestinians. There has been little peace in the area since.

The third factor—money—is, of course, linked to the first: within the next few decades the moguls of the Middle East could, some fear, have accumulated enough money from the marketing of oil to dominate if not control the financial world.

CHAPTER **II**

Oil of the Middle East

THE story behind the White House meeting in October, 1973, of the oil embargo and resultant shortage—the whole story of oil in the Middle East—is vastly intriguing. It is also vastly complicated.

It involves intimately two of the most exclusive clubs in the world. One is OPEC, the Organization of Petroleum Exporting Countries. OPEC has twelve members (and one associate) and eight of them are countries of the Middle East. The eight own and control by far the major portion of oil produced by OPEC members.

Members of the other club are the Seven Sisters of the oil industry: Exxon, Gulf, Mobil, Socal (Standard Oil of California), Texaco, British Petroleum (BP), and Shell. The first five are American, descendants of John D. Rockefeller's original Standard Oil. BP is, of course, British, and Shell is predominantly of the Netherlands.

The phrase "Seven Sisters" for the seven giants of the oil world originated within the industry (most probably from a spiteful independent) and was so obviously appropriate that it stuck. The Seven Sisters, through either their own production or purchase, control the original basic crude oil, the transport, the refining, and the marketing of at least a third of the world's oil. Also the decisions as to when and where to explore.

Like sisters, the seven compete for perquisites within their megatherian industry, but they also trade confidences and courtesies, and, faced with an external threat, they cling tightly together and present a solid, solid front to the common enemy.

There were and are also, of course, a number of independent oil companies dealing in the Middle East—American, European, and Japanese. Compared to the Sisters, however, the independents are very small potatoes and usually have been content (or compelled) to follow whatever leads the Sisters established.

The Middle Eastern members of OPEC are Saudi Arabia, Kuwait, Iraq, Qatar, the United Arab Emirates, Algeria, Libya, and Iran. Neither war nor peace, famine or flood has been able to unite the Arab nations (only Iran of the above is not Arab). The solid front is still tenuous. In early 1977 Saudi Arabia and the Emirates broke with the others in OPEC on a price rise.

In the early years of oil exploration and conquest in the Middle East, the Seven Sisters made their deals with the various governments for whatever bargains they could wring. Implanted visions of Rolls Royces and private planes for Arab rulers didn't hurt the Sisters' bargaining power, and the royalties they doled out varied; none could be called overgenerous.

Then, in the 1930s, South America's Venezuela, a recently oil rich nation whose oil was being extracted by three of the Sisters—Exxon, Shell, and Gulf—began demanding a greater share of oil profits and the demands were made under the threat of nationalization.

They ultimately won their battle. The Middle Eastern nations, which had been watching the action closely, followed suit and by mid-century the fifty-fifty split emerged. And also the posted price.

Greatly simplified, the two factors worked like this: the oil companies agreed to stop fuzzing up the prices they were selling their products for and to establish a "posted price" at the well. This would be the selling price to anyone who wanted to buy. The "fifty-fifty split" simply meant that the country government would get 50 percent of this posted price from the oil companies.

Of course, the Sisters had a twist and it came in a tax deal. With the consent of the U.S. State Department and Bureau of Internal Revenue, the 50 percent partnership rate paid to the oil country was declared to be an income tax to that government and hence not taxable in this country. The American government raitonalized the act as a variety of foreign aid, and the oil companies happily kept increasing their oil investments abroad and paying no American taxes on the profits.

Things rocked along on this basis for a number of years until 1959 when some of the Seven Sisters, fearful of a glut in the oil market and vastly underestimating the demand over the next few years, began cutting prices at the wellhead. Enraged and alarmed at this development, five of the world's leading oil countries convened a meeting in Baghdad in September, 1959.

The nations represented were Iran, Iraq, Saudi Arabia,

Kuwait, and Venezuela. At the meeting they resolved that fluctuations in oil prices were affecting the stability of both the exporting and consuming nations and that the producing nations must be consulted on any changes in prices. And they agreed among themselves, for the first time, that the oil producers must present a solid front to the Seven Sisters: a cartel to meet a cartel, in effect. And there in Baghdad they organized OPEC, the Organization of Petroleum Exporting Countries.

With OPEC also came the idea of "participation," that is, a partnership between the oil governments and the oil companies. Foremost in the slowly evolving demand from the Middle East for a share in decision-making was Sheikh Zaki Yamani, the Oil Minister of Saudi Arabia. A graduate of Harvard, Yamani had been in his post since 1962, gradually increasing his influence with his king and expanding his power base through his bright intelligence, his ability to cut through the fog of technical jargon, and his skill at the negotiating table. In his years of representing the largest oil-producing nation, Sheikh Yamani has gained a certain reputation, enhanced by the curly dark hair and the short, pointed beard. Few missed the Mephistophelean air which he cultivated with some amusement.

Sheikh Yamani preached a theme that the oil-producing countries must know what is going on in the oil business world and that they must have a say in the decisions. The thought did not originate with Yamani, but he was its most persistent and successful prosecutor.

Along with about everything else in the world, the price of crude oil had been creeping up, always under the strict control of the oil companies. By 1971, however, the idea of participation had become a firm fixation with the Middle Eastern producers; they also were quite competent to observe that the increases they received were by no means keeping up with the worldwide rate of inflation in the products they imported from the West.

By this time OPEC had enlarged its status to the point that it felt quite able to confront the Seven Sisters. Satisfied of that, in early 1971, OPEC made certain price demands on the oil companies and when their demands were not met, signed the Tehran Agreement. The date was February 14, St. Valentine's Day. It escalated the price by thirty cents a barrel, to be increased up to fifty cents by 1975. Compared to the price rises of two years later, this increase nows seems petty. The oil companies felt it was calamitous, more perhaps because they sensed that it signaled the beginning erosion of their control than for the actual money.

They were eminently correct. At a June meeting of OPEC that same year the members voted to demand direct shares in the oil operations of their nations: 20 percent immediately, increasing to 51 percent over a period of years. The shares they acquired would be paid for at the "net book value," that is, the value placed on those shares by the companies themselves.

By this time the original five members of OPEC had been increased and the total included: Iraq, Saudi Arabia, Kuwait, Qatar, the United Arab Emirates, Algeria, Iran, Libya, Ecuador, Venezuela, Indonesia, Nigeria, and Gabon (an associate). Forming an organization within an organization, the first five of the countries named above united into OAPEC or the Organization of Arab Petroleum Exporting Countries. All of these nations border on the Persian Gulf. (Iran does, too, but Iran is Persian, not Arab.)

The stand against the oil companies, which quickly escalated into combat proportions with conferences, debates, arguments, and accusations, went on through 1972 until October when, with Sheikh Yamani heading the Arab negotiators, the members of OAPEC reached an agreement with the oil companies. By this time, however, the percentage had increased. The agreement called for the producing countries to acquire 51 percent of the concessions by 1983, with 25 percent to be purchased immediately. This was the opening wedge and provided a model pact for the other oil nations to follow.

This controversy was quickly followed by another over the "buy-back price" of the portion of oil which went to the producing countries. Under the threat of cutbacks, which would automatically reduce the available supply of oil, the Sisters agreed to a "buy-back price" of 93 percent of the posted price. OPEC was now firmly in the driver's seat and the reign of the Seven Sisters was ended—or at least mitigated. Or so it seemed at the time.

During the early 1970s another factor had crept into the already frightening oil picture. The oil companies, honestly or in an attempt to curb overproduction and thus cause lower prices, had greatly underestimated both the national and the global demand for crude oil. They also had overestimated production in the United States, which meant that this country would have to import more and export less. Which it continued to do.

The summer of 1973 was nightmarish for the oil companies. The demand for oil worldwide exceeded all of the highest predictions, and with it came a scramble from both independents and Sisters for the Arab share of crude at the well. In the meantime, the members of OPEC moved closer in their unification and, at this point, in their determination to use their oil as a weapon against Israel. Even Saudi Arabia's King Faisal, whose traditional friendship to the United States had been counted on as a countering force against the other Middle East oil nations, was now making it dangerously clear that he would not stand alone against his brethren. In June, OPEC negotiated a 12 percent price raise and Saudi Arabia's Yamani warned the oil companies that this would probably be the last negotiation; hereafter, he said, the members of OPEC would simply set their own prices and the Seven Sisters could meet them or do without. In August, 1973, Libya nationalized 51 percent of all oil companies operating in that country: Exxon, Mobil, Texaco, Socal, and Shell. At least one independent company had already been nationalized. The old order had changed. Now it was no longer that oil must find a market, but that the market must find oil.

Then, on October 6, 1973, the fourth and biggest of the Arab-Israeli wars erupted along the Suez Canal and on the Golan Heights, with both Syria and Egypt invading Israeli-occupied territory. A meeting between the OAPEC countries plus Iran and a team of five negotiators from the

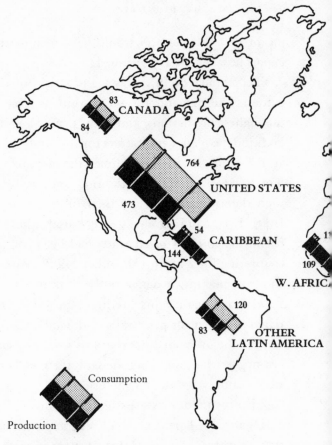

Figures in million metric tons courtesy of
British Petroleum Statistical Review 1975

Sisters met in Vienna two days later. The oil men refused
to meet the price demands and the meeting broke up,
the oil officials returning to consult their company boards
and the OPEC members simply adjourning to Kuwait.

There the oil companies agreed, without consultation
with the Seven Sisters, to raise the price of crude oil from
the $3 a barrel agreed to at the Tehran meeting to $5.12
a barrel, a jump of 70 percent, plus an immediate cutback

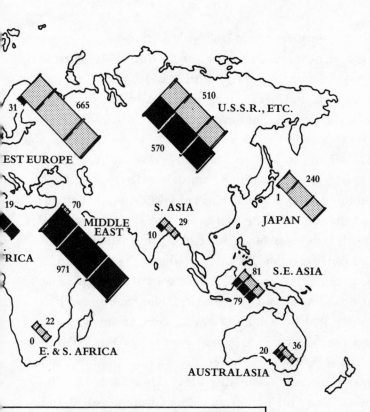

31 665

510 U.S.S.R., ETC.

EST EUROPE

570

19 70 S. ASIA 240
1
MIDDLE 29 JAPAN
EAST 10

RICA 0
971 81 S.E. ASIA

79

22
0

E. & S. AFRICA 20 36

AUSTRALASIA

OIL SUPPLY AND DEMAND

in production of 5 percent, along with the warning that
an equal monthly cutback would be applied until Israel
had withdrawn from occupied territories.

Then came the White House meeting and the rebuff
dealt to Saudi Arabia's Omar Saqqaf and the other three
Arabian foreign ministers. That was on October 17, 1973,
and on October 20 King Faisal announced his boycott,
coupled with a *10 percent* cutback in production. The

other oil countries fell in line with the boycott.

Late in October a cessation of hostilities was effected and negotiations on Israel's withdrawal began. The tension relaxed and before long the total embargo was relaxed. The cutbacks, however, continued. So did the lines of cars at American service stations.

The arguments between the members of OPEC on a yet new price for oil continued until late December, 1973, when the Persian Gulf members of OPEC met in Tehran. When the smoke of the conference had cleared away, the Shah of Iran, host of the meeting, presented the world with a Christmas gift. He announced that the six countries had agreed on a price of $11.65 a barrel, which more than doubled the old posted price. The Shah noted that the price had been far too low in comparison with the things the Middle East bought from the West. Western children were assured of three meals a day, he noted, and he hoped for that eventuality for children of the Middle East, too. The oil importing nations were appalled and helpless to do anything except pay the new price.

It wasn't the best time for it to have happened, but about this date the oil companies announced their profits for the third quarter of 1973, as follows: Exxon, $638 million, up 80 percent; Texaco, $307 million, up 48 percent; Mobil, $231 million, up 64 percent; and Gulf, $210 million, up 91 percent; and on throughout the list.

CHAPTER **III**

Politics of the Middle East

THE Mediterranean, said Emil Ludwig, is the Helen among oceans. Like her, it has been desired by all who saw her. More recently, Jesse Lewis, in his book for Foreign Affairs Study, wrote: "In many ways the Mediterranean is a barometer of the world's political climate. This is more true today than at any other time in modern history because developments in the Mediterranean countries and the state of relations among them often mirror the state of relations of the two super-powers."

There are fifteen nations with coastlines on the Mediterranean and nine of those are of the Middle East and North Africa. (There also are two island countries: Malta and Cyprus.)

These nine countries for the past several years now have been at the center of world politics as well as the world economy. They comprise a big share of the Middle East and have, at one time or another, maintained its well-rated reputation as a trouble spot, target for intrigue as well as vortex of it, notable for plot and counterplot, assassination, local wars—all coupled with an awesome and worrisome latter-day arms buildup.

The arms buildup is competitive and deadly, because of the potential for trouble-making it encourages. The weapons are not outdated castoffs of the big powers, but modern and ultrasophisticated: Iran's Grumman F-14 Tomcat and Israel's F-15, made by McDonnell Douglas, vie with the Soviet Mig-23 bought by Egypt and Syria.

Matching this modern airpower are the missiles, tanks, and artillery bought and ready for use—once in a while to the point of the absurd, as the purchase by tiny Abu Dhabi (one of the Emirates) of five French-made Mirage 5 fighter planes to protect the lives and territory of its sixty thousand people. Iran has also flirted with buying a $500 million border surveillance system.

The news of the past few years has not been all bad for Middle East internal affairs. Turkey in the far north has reached at least a stalemate in the Cyprus confrontation, Iran and Iraq agreed to settle their border differences off the field of battle, and Iraq and Saudi Arabia negotiated a compromise on territorial rights over the neutral zone lying between the two oil powers. Other events, however, have been less felicific.

The two situations in the Middle East which have held the attention of the world for the past few years, of course, are the Arab-Israeli wars and the brutal destructive fighting in Lebanon, which began as a civil war. The troubles of Israel and her neighbors continue to pose the greatest threat to world peace through the chance of involving the superpowers. The fighting in Lebanon, as it accelerated in intensity and firepower, also began to involve its neighbors, but never actually posed the threat Israel has. Both situations are complicated.

In the turgid Lebanon script there are three basic spheres of conflict:

1. Age-old rivalries between religious groups and feudal political leaders.
2. The left-right conflict between radicals and conservatives.
3. The bitter antagonism between the Lebanese Nationalists and the Palestinian *fedayeen* or commandos.

Further adding to this complexity is the political organization of Lebanon itself. The country has a population of three million people. Theoretically the population is 51 percent Christian and 49 percent Muslim. Predicated on this assumption, the government is organized to always have a Christian President, a Muslim Prime Minister, and a parliament divided six to five in favor of the Christians.

That population division may have been true once. Today it is not. Probably about 15 percent of the population of Lebanon is Palestinian, largely Muslim although many are not citizens of Lebanon, and of the remainder a clear majority of the people are Muslim, probably between 65 and 70 percent.

Both Christian and Muslim groups in the country are subdivided into smaller units. The largest of the Christian faiths are the Maronites, with Greek Orthodox, Armenians, and other sects trailing in dimension. The Muslims are divided among the Sunni, or professed orthodox, and some fewer Druze (who are not technically Muslims but have sided with them).

Nor is that the end of the complications. Superimposed on the religious picture is the left-right, liberal-conservative confrontation. The Maronites, with a few other Christian sects, form the bulk of the conservative right. Also included are a few moderate Muslims. The liberal left (radical, if you prefer) is composed of less moderate Muslims, Druze, Greek Orthodox, and Armenian Christians. Thus, the struggle is not simply a matter of Muslim against Christian; it is also right against left.

Speaking before the American Society of International Law, former Under Secretary of State (now President of American University) Joseph Sisco, said: "The Left has for many years been striving for a restructuring of the Lebanese system. It has built its strength in large part on the aspirations of the poor people—notably the Muslims—who have moved into Beirut and other cities in the last thirty years. These people have seen the wealth of the city predominantly in Christian hands and they have felt that they were not getting their fair share.

"When we read in today's newspapers that the urban gunmen, who come from these underprivileged groups, are so heavily involved, you can understand that they shed no tears over the destruction of the luxury hotels which represent for them a life style in which they did not participate."

The third dimension in the Lebanese civil war, as noted earlier, was the Palestinian *fedayeen*-Lebanese Nationalist factor. Since the late 1960s the commandos had become more and more powerful, controlling not only the refugee camps from which they drew their support and recruits, but also gradually exerting an arrogant sovereignty over the surrounding territory as well. And the more the *fedayeen* flexed their muscles, the more they annoyed the nationalistic-minded Lebanese, to the point of armed clashes with Lebanese Army units on several occasions.

By late 1976, after nineteen months of bitter fighting and 40,000 deaths in the civil war, the other Arab nations belatedly decided to step in. Syrian armored columns, only recently themselves involved in the fighting, became the spearhead of an Arab League peace-keeping force planned to reach some 30,000 troops and to include forces from the Sudan, Saudi Arabia, and other Arab nations. A negotiated peace was to follow.

Within a few days the roads to Beirut, Tripoli, and Sidon were cleared and fighting throughout the interior of the country had stopped. The peace-keeping force was welcomed by the Muslim leftists and regarded with suspicion by the Christian rightists. The short strip of border between Lebanon and Israel, so often a trouble spot in the past, showed few signs of change. Israel warned of trouble if either Palestinian or Syrian troops were placed on duty there.

And now to Israel and her neighbors.

The first Arab-Israeli war began immediately after the State of Israel was formally created on May 14, 1948, and is known to the Israelis as their "War of Independence."

That same day, Arab armies from Egypt, Jordan, Iraq, Syria, and Lebanon moved into the sectors of Palestine which had not been apportioned to the Jews, as a prelude to a general attack. Their first actual hostile action was to take and hold the small part of the Old City of Jerusalem, which had been allocated to the Jews. Meanwhile the quickly mobilized Jewish forces moved, too, through the hills of Judah in the south. They took charge of the main road to Jerusalem, beating back Arab attacks, and by early 1949 controlled almost the entire Negev (the area bordering the Sinai Peninsula and Jordan; they did not control the Gaza Strip).

Early in 1949 armistice negotiations were begun which culminated in July with an agreement whereby the Israelis established, on a "temporary basis," their frontiers at the point they had been when the negotiations began. Which, of course, resulted in a considerably expanded State of Israel.

The United Nations, in creating Israel, had envisioned two states, one Arab, the other Israeli, with Jerusalem—which Arabs and Jews both claim as a shrine—an open, international enclave. It never quite worked out that way and after the 1948 war, in which the warring forces fought over the city, it still remained under a divided control.

There was never a real relaxation of the tension, and Israel was kept busy defending the lands she occupied, mostly from small-scale commando raids and terrorist activities.

On July 26, 1956, Gamal Abdel Nasser, the late president and strong man of Egypt, seized control of, and declared his intention to nationalize, the European-built-and-owned Suez Canal, the vital waterway which links the Red Sea with the Mediterranean. This, as can be imagined, sent England and France into a united foaming rage, coupled with threats of war or something near it, and brought American President Dwight D. Eisenhower galloping in as peacemaker.

Under the threat of armed invasion from Britain and France, Nasser withdrew his troops from the Sinai Peninsula to defend the canal and its environs. Then, as the tension mounted and both France and England busied themselves with militant threats, the Israeli armed forces moved into the Sinai vacuum to destroy hostile bases there—perhaps at British-French request, perhaps because it seemed an ideal time to take advantage of an enemy who was occupied elsewhere.

In less than a week the virtually unopposed Jewish forces captured the Gaza Strip on the Mediterranean, the city of Gaza, and the city of El-'Arish, which lies on the Mediterranean between Gaza and Port Said. They also took thousands of prisoners and occupied parts of the Sinai clear up to the canal itself; and they gained control over the Gulf of Aqaba, which gave them an outlet to the Red Sea and posed yet another threat to Egypt.

After a number of conferences, massive peace-laden intervention from the United States and the United Nations, France and England bowed to the inevitability of the canal's nationalization, Israel withdrew to her earlier lines of conquest, and the crisis subsided.

The next ten years saw the by-now-normal uneasy peace between Israel and her Arab neighbors. Then, in late May of 1967, Egypt's Nasser closed the Strait of Tiran at the mouth of Aqaba, effectively cutting off Israel's access to the Red Sea. Despite protests from the United States and other nations that the Straits were international waters, Nasser stuck to his guns, such as they were, cheered on by his Arab neighbors who had accused him of weakness in dealing with the Israelis. Nasser had previously effected the removal of the UN peacekeeping force and moved a sizeable force of Egyptian troops to the Israel border. Syria and Jordan were promised partners in any military action which might be forthcoming.

The Israeli Air Force, like the rest of the nation's forces, was under command of the Minister of Defense, Major General Moshe Dayan, who had his forces on ready alert from June 1, but did not act until June 5. Then at 7:45 A.M., he struck with his four hundred fighter bombers. They attacked ten Egyptian airfields simultaneously in waves ten minutes apart, flying at tree-top level to evade Egyptian radar. Three hours later the Egyptian Air Force ceased to exist as a fighting force. Most of the planes were destroyed on the ground, often as they attempted to take off. In many cases, their pilots died at the controls. Later in the day the Israeli pilots destroyed the Syrian Air Force and then the Jordanian.

The Jewish ground forces were equally successful and by June 10, when the Six-Day War had ended, the Arabs had lost the Sinai Peninsula, the Old City of Jerusalem, the Gaza Strip, the West Bank (i.e., the Jordanian territory west of the River Jordan), and the Golan Heights on the Syrian border. During the course of the Six-Day War the Egyptians mined, blocked, and closed the Suez Canal and it remained so for two years.

Future histories of the Middle East will treat the Arab-Israeli struggles as one war which lasted for a quarter century—or longer, should there be more—with brief interludes when the hostilities subsided to mere guerrilla harassment.

The fourth in the series of major hostilities is now known as the Yom Kippur War. It started with a surprise attack by the Egyptians on the Israel positions in the Sinai bordering the canal. The attack came on October 6, 1973, the Jewish Day of Atonement—Yom Kippur—a major religious holiday, and was paralleled by the Arab oil boycott, although which, war or boycott, was cause and which effect may not be known positively for some years. Certainly Egypt's President Anwar Sadat, who succeeded to the top office after Nasser's death on September 28, 1970, had labored long and hard to convince the Arab oil-producing states that their oil was a weapon and should be so used.

The attack caught the Jews off balance and was greatly successful for the Egyptians in its first phase. By midnight on the first day, four hundred tanks had crossed the canal, circled and outflanked the Jewish lines. Simultaneously Syrian tank forces had struck the Golan Heights with initial success.

The fighting continued for three weeks (disregarding several UN-proposed cease-fires). The conclusion came after the application of firm pressure, applied by the United States and the nations of Europe who were themselves under the pressure of the growing oil shortage and a cold winter ahead. By that time the Israeli forces had taken the offensive and driven back both the Egyptian and Syrian forces, occupying additional Syrian territory, several bridgeheads across the canal, and were threatening the city of Damascus, some fifty miles below the Golan Heights on Israel's northeastern border. The Arabs and particularly President Sadat, however, had achieved their main objectives. They proved that the Israeli armies were not invincible and that oil could be an effective weapon when used collectively, as it could and probably will be hereafter. Thus, under the Disengagement Agreement, which Egypt and Israel signed on January 18, 1974, the Jewish forces pulled back from ten to fifteen miles from the canal, establishing a neutral zone under control of a UN peace-keeping force, and left all Syrian soil.

None of the four Arab-Israeli wars, of course, accomplished anything to mitigate their chief cause—the refugees from the lands now occupied by the Jews, known as something the rest of the world would prefer to forget, and universally ignored as the "Palestine Problem."

In 1947, the British, who were the actual originators of the plan and who had promised to provide the Jews of the world with a homeland, referred the "Palestine Question" to the United Nations. There, of course, the General Assembly approved a plan to partition Palestine into two states, one Jewish and one Arab. The area allotted the Jews was greatly enlarged by their War of Independence the following year, and the Arabs displaced by the new Israeli nation settled in camps in Jordan, Lebanon, Syria, and Egypt—save a few who migrated to the United States or other foreign countries.

The camps were established as temporary, and originally for some 800,000 men, women, and children. They have existed now, and not exactly as showplaces, for more than twenty-five years, and they have grown enormously throughout the years, particularly after each of the successive wars.

The Arab nations of the Middle East do not accept Israel as a legitimate entity, nor do the refugees. And it is from these Arab refugee camps, largely, that come the bitter, angry people, many of them a new generation who know no other life, to make up most of the guerrilla and terrorist groups carrying out a sporadic warfare against the Jews and the Jewish movement. For them it has become a form of holy warfare.

CHAPTER **IV**

The Petrobillions

THE increase in the oil revenues of the Middle East oil-producing countries in the first half of the 1970 decade was dramatic enough to satisfy the demands of all melodrama. At the beginning of the decade, in 1970, the combined revenues of all the Persian Gulf countries was just over $4 billion. The price of oil at the wellhead was less than twenty cents per barrel.

By the year 1974, after the Tehran Agreement, after the blockade and after the cutbacks, the Arabs had taken a firm control over their oil. The price had risen to more than $11 a barrel and the total annual oil revenue to the Persian Gulf countries alone was almost $85 billion.

It is widely believed in the oil industry today that by 1980 the price of crude oil will have climbed up to $12 and, with slight increases in production, those same states will have a combined oil income of $100 billion.

As the huge increases in the oil revenues of the Gulf nations (none of the oil figures in this chapter will include productions or revenues to the North African nations) became known, economists of the world quite naturally began speculation as to possible uses to which such a vast sum as $100 billion could be put.

And, immediately, those in the United States came up

with some figures which were enough to startle the financial world. For instance, with only a little more than half of that $100 billion, the oil nations of the Persian Gulf could buy up all of the outstanding stock of General Motors, General Electric, Exxon, Ford Motors, Chrysler, Texaco, and Mobil.

Actually they could have bought those companies in 1974 when their oil revenues were slightly over $50 billion. And the next year they could have bought IBM, ITT, Gulf, Socal, Western Electric, Westinghouse, U.S. Steel, RCA, and half a dozen other giant American corporations.

And, presumably, in succeeding years with added purchases, they would have in effect bought the United States.

All of these facts were frightening. To bring home the power of all these petrobillions, Michael Fields, in his book, *A Hundred Million Dollars a Day*, noted that by 1980, Saudi Arabia alone would be able to finance the research and development costs of a supersonic Concorde with its oil production revenues for just about one month.

About this time several events became public news through the press. Giant ITT borrowed $100 million through bonds sold to the Arabs. Iran attempted to loan the Grumman Company, makers of the ultramodern F-14 fighter plane, $100 million or more, and actually did contribute $75 million to a bank consortium loan of $200 million to the financially troubled company. Iran also attempted, for a time, to become a major stockholder in Pan American, which in the event of an emergency becomes an important part of the Defense Department's reserve fleet.

The biggest shock of all came, however, when the *Washington Post* reported rumors that Arab investors had attempted to buy a major chunk of Lockheed, the giant defense contractor.

After reading the story, Senator Daniel Inouye of Hawaii, a member of the Aviation Subcommittee of the Senate Commerce Committee, wrote a letter to then Secretary of Defense James Schlesinger concerning the story. Part of their question-and-answer exchange, taken from the February 18, 1975, *Congressional Record*, reads:

Q. Is the Department of Defense able to confirm the report that an offer for a controlling interest in Lockheed was in fact made by Arab investors?

A. The Department of Defense has no information other than what has appeared in the news media.

Q. Is the Department able to confirm the claim that Lockheed rejected the offer in the manner described in the *Post* article?

A. The Department is not familiar with the action taken by Lockheed or the relationship described in the *Post* article.

Q. If such an offer was made, was the Department advised of it? At what point was the Department told of the offer and the rejection?

A. The Department has received no information on the reported offer and rejection.

Q. If such offers for control are made, does the Department require this information to be forwarded to the Department? If not, why not? If yes, at what point during the negotiation would this information have to be provided to the Department?

A. Under the Defense Industrial Security Program, cleared Defense contractors are required to report when such offers become accepted and as a result a change of ownership occurred to an extent that control of a corporation was affected. Furthermore, should foreign interests own or become owners of 6 percent or more of the corporation's voting stock, we are furnished a report of such changed conditions in accordance with paragraph 6a (4) of the Industrial Security Manual for Safeguarding Classified Information, together with a revised Certificate Pertaining to Foreign Affiliation.

The offer had been made, and had been rejected by Lockheed. This fact, coupled with the other proposals of one kind or another which had been coming along and the publicity given them, sent Congress to examining its laws covering foreign acquisitions of American companies.

They learned from Secretary Schlesinger's replies to Senator Inouye that the Defense Department, and presumably the Office of the President, would be advised, if not before, at least after a 6 percent acquisition of ownership by foreign nationals. And, digging deeper into their own laws, Congress found that under the Communications Act of 1934, all communications companies are sharply restricted to a 20 percent foreign ownership either by purchase or merger. A communications company is defined as a company which requires a radio license to operate. This covers, of course, a wide range of business: all commercial radio and television broadcasting companies, all of the several hundred American telephone companies, Western Union—everything from satellite to walkie-talkie communication.

There were, in addition, several bills designed to strengthen the control over the stock of American corporations, including one by Senator Harrison A. Williams of New Jersey. His bill, S. 425, as he defined it is "primarily concerned with the problems posed by foreign investment in this country. But, in addition, S. 425 would require all issuers of publicly traded securities to maintain and make public the names, residences, and nationalities of all beneficial owners of their equity securities. The bill would thus provide a comprehensive scheme for the disclosure of the ownership and control of American business. This and several other similar measures were pending in 1977.

On the other hand, the American government, along with American businessmen, has always welcomed foreign investment and only gets concerned when it hits sensitive areas. As one government official put it: "We would be delighted to have the Arab oil people come in and buy into Quaker Oats."

And there has been a lot of Arab oil money invested in nonsensitive areas of America. Something like $11 billion in oil money poured into the United States in 1974. Of this, about $6 billion went into government bonds, a favorite spot of Arab investors, $4 billion into bank deposits (all short term, usually under six months), and only $1 billion into corporate stocks and bonds. The sum was probably equalled in 1975, plus various investments made by European banks with funds entrusted to them by Arab investors.

There were also sporadic purchases and attempted purchases made by individual investors, mostly banks and real estate, both favorites for Arab financial portfolios. In 1975, a group of royal Kuwait investors attempted to buy the 108-year-old National Savings and Trust Company in Washington, D.C., a bank which just happens to be across the street from the U.S. Treasury Building. The bank declined to sell. Arab investors also failed in an attempt to buy the First National Bank in San Jose, California, but did pick up a one-third interest in the Michigan Bank of the Commonwealth, which has around $900 million in deposits. Another Kuwait group overcame the protests of environmentalists to acquire and develop Kiawah Island, connected to the mainland of South Carolina by a causeway and only thirty-five miles from Charleston. The first ten town houses to go up sold immediately for $150,000 each, with much more extensive development scheduled for 1977 and the years following. The beach there is one of the loveliest on the Atlantic coast.

Saudi Arabia, in mid-1976, bought a building just across the street from the State Department in Washington's Foggy Bottom for a price "in excess of $1 million," reportedly to be for the office of the Saudi Arabian Armed Forces attache. It is a medium-sized structure and undoubtedly will be used for other Saudi Arabian government offices as well, but such scattering of space by foreign governments is common enough in Washington—and most other capitals.

Late in June, 1976, the Occidental Oil Company, one of the majors but not quite in the class of the Seven Sisters, agreed to sell 10 percent of its stock to Iran for $125 million. The deal, which is similar to Iran's purchase the year before of 25 percent of the giant German Krupp Works steel division, gave Iran 6.2 million shares of Occidental, an option on a similar amount, and one seat on the Board of Directors. The option is good for five years.

The financial apprehensions engendered by the scary headlines abated over the next several years when there were few, if any, signs of obsessive Arab interest shown in American investments. And, on the other hand, Arabian oil is not really draining all that much of the nation's wealth.

Spurred into action by the possibilities of the situation, the Commerce Department commissioned a study, and in mid-1976 released all nine volumes and 2,500 pages of it.

"The concern over massive foreign takeovers of U.S. industries, especially by the Middle East oil-producing countries, is unsubstantiated," Commerce said, and went on to cite facts and figures:

All foreign investment in the United States in the form of direct ownership totals between $25 and $30 billion. This amounts to about 3.5 percent of all United States investments (not including housing).

Britain, Holland, and Canada have the largest investment holdings in the United States. They are trailed by

Japan, some other European countries—and then the oil nations.

The labor force dependent on foreign investments in the United States is less than a million and a quarter people. This is less than 2 percent of the total force.

Of the oil-producing nations, Venezuela in South America has the most extensive investments here.

The report did urge Congress to provide additional authority for monitoring foreign investments.

Where do the Arab petrodollars go? A lot of them get spent right at home. The Arabs, and quite naturally, are concerned first with themselves and their own countries. Kuwait went from rags to riches, from one of the world's poorest nations to one of its richest, and to a life, also, as one of the world's most lavishly endowed welfare states. All of the Arab oil nations spent millions of their oil dollars on schools, roads, hospitals, electrical systems, and other internal infrastructural improvements. Some looked a little into the future. Dubai, one of the Emirates, for instance, went heavily into public works, including an airport large enough to let three giant jet airliners land simultaneously. The total population of Dubai is less than seventy thousand people.

And, as businessmen, the Arabs also established within their own borders factories and factory complexes which would be productive of both incomes and employment: cement factories, fertilizer plants, oil refineries, fish packing and canning facilities—and light industries of half a dozen varieties.

A lot of Arab dollars went for land speculation. In their own countries selling and buying of land was used by some governments as a way of spreading the wealth, i.e., permitting the sale of public lands at low prices and then repurchasing (by government) at high prices. In foreign countries—mostly Europe—the individual oil moguls have bought apartment houses, houses, estates, penthouses, villas, and whatever.

In the United States they dabbled in Florida real estate and some found themselves in the same situation as many American investors: not losers, for, in a sense, all land purchase is potentially sound, but now becoming aware that it may be years and years before development catches up with location and their investments can be cashed in. Of course, the Arab, in a sense, is quite like the average Middle Westerner in America; he likes land because he understands it. It is a tangible thing he can see and touch, and he would much rather own a farm in Kuwait or a country estate in England than an infinitesimal part of a large corporation through the purchase of its stock.

And, of course, a certain amount of the millions of oil dollars go for the material things in life and to the immediate benefit of the "royal families" of the Middle East. One government official, whose high office in government gives him access to the national treasury, spends several months a year in Paris and considers it normal to withdraw seven to eight hundred thousand dollars in funds to pay his expenses during the stay. His brethren, if not legion, are at least numerous.

Others travel to other places. Children—and in the collective families they reach a considerable number—are almost always educated abroad with liberal allowances. A few return to help out in their governments; most prefer to go into business, and a few follow a well-known Western custom of becoming perpetual students.

There are rather high national expenditures for such personal creature comforts as private jet aircraft, custom-built motor cars, palaces, and an occasional yacht. The cocktail conversation in oil circles abounds with stories, some tall, some laughable. One, almost certainly apocryphal, tells of the sheikh of one of the smaller and more tightly held kingdoms, who complained bitterly that the money printed in England attracted mice. They had nibbled away some £50,000 he had stored temporarily in the cellar.

One transition the Middle East oil nations have made is into a belated consciousness of improving the picture they, as nations and people, present to the rest of the world. This is probably more emphasized in America—where image-selling is a way of life—than in the rest of the world.

They have engineered this on several levels: by employing public relations firms, Washington lobbyists—usually former high government officials—and by sending ambassadors to the Washington embassies who have been educated at Ivy League schools, have lived and even worked in New York or Washington, and who know their way around both in American business and in power politics.

The lobbyists, usually employed through the American law firms of which they are members, included such well-

known figures as former Senator J. William Fulbright
(United Arab Emirates); Richard Kleindienst, who
achieved some notoriety as Attorney General for President Nixon, and Clark Clifford, former Secretary of Defense (both Algeria); and Frederick G. Dutton, one of the
Kennedy advisors (Saudi Arabia).

Functioning nationwide reportedly is an extensive
propaganda or public relations (take your choice) program
laid out to persuade Americans to give the Arabs at least
an even break with the Israelis in their opinions, personal,
political, and business. An Arab Information Center has
been established with offices in New York, Washington,
Chicago, Dallas, and San Francisco. It publishes a bi-
weekly *Arab Report* whose language is so intemperate it
is more liable to repel than attract friends for the Arab
countries. It also has been in trouble with the Justice Department at least once on charges of violating the Foreign
Agents Registration Act.

Most effective of all the efforts to enhance the public
image of the Middle East nations has been in Washington
by the ambassadors. In some cases these are the new
breed. Sometimes they are the old-timers who have simply
undergone a change of attitude. Once the ranking members of most Middle Eastern embassies could hardly have
found their ways to Capitol Hill and they limited their
American political contacts to the State Department. They
had little time for the media and rarely returned a press
query. They didn't scorn the public; it simply didn't exist
for them.

Now, in addition to the lobbyists who guide them

through both the halls of Congress and the maze of politics, they have, in some instances, established public information offices in their chanceries. Instead of the once-a-year big bashes where everything was impersonal, they now hold smaller, more intimate, affairs where there is a chance for quiet conversation and the guests are influential political figures and the top columnists or television figures. They also work hard to get public figures to tour their countries—personages like Senators Charles Percy, Edward Kennedy, Thomas Eagleton, Adlai Stevenson III, and George McGovern, all of whom went, (not to mention Elizabeth Taylor).

The publicity campaign and the quieter work of the lobbyists do not come cheaply and the press has, on occasion, made much of this side of the story: the wild spending for influence.

Money is involved, of course, and the individual lobbyist fees ($200,000 a year, $700,000 a year) sound high, as does, say, $15 million for a publicity campaign. Actually, all of the money paid by all of the Arab states to all of their lobbyists in Washington would not approach, probably, the amount of money either Presidential candidate spent in 1976. And the $15 million paid for a public relations campaign? The Department of Defense spends several times that amount annually to sell America's own military, just to America.

CHAPTER V

The Sumerians

Hɪsᴛᴏʀʏ began when man first paused in his wanderings for a night, a season, or a century, and, intentionally or otherwise, left indelible records in the dust and ashes or on the walls of his halting places.

In terms of time for these recorded bivouacs, the Middle East is ancient, ancient. Man, or his erect immediate ancestor, has probably lived on earth for a million and a half or more years, but he has left unmistakable evidence of his life and its style in the Middle East longer than anywhere else yet discovered: from twelve to ten thousand years.

It is nearly five hundred years ago that Columbus discovered the world of the Americas. In a narrative world history written of all twelve thousand years at some future date, the era from 1492 to the present would be compressed into a couple of paragraphs, probably devoted to the beginning of the mechanical age and the contrivance of the atomic bomb.

Up until the 1920s the world knew little about its own history earlier than some three thousand years before Christ. Many earlier diggers into the ancient cities— Ninevah, Babylon, Dur-Sharrukin and others—had not been interested in piecing together a fabric of history but in finding artifacts for the museums (who sponsored the digs) or just for sale, if they were excavating on their own. In their carelessness with picks, shovels, and battering rams, these early predators ruined many sites (and thousands of artifacts) for the serious archaeologists and anthropologists who came later.

Today's explorers are interested in artifacts too, of course, but for what the artifacts can tell them in terms of history—not price. They excavate with trowels and spoons, not shovels, and they employ modern techniques. A photograph taken by an aerial camera will frequently outline the borders of a long-buried city, and even mark certain recognizable areas within. Nuclear techniques are used to date carbon content to determine ages. Mine detectors locate buried artifacts. Layers of the past are peeled back, carefully, inch by inch by inch.

History is always open to the revelations of later finds, but evidence thus far uncovered marks that area of what once was Mesopotamia and is now Iraq—which the Greeks named the "Land Between the Rivers"—as the area where man first stopped in his wanderings, learned to grow his food and domesticate animals, and emerged eventually into what we call civilization.

The rivers are, of course, the Tigris and the Euphrates, whose alluvial deposits provided fertile soil and whose waters were a source of the first agricultural irrigation. The first man came to the "Land Between the Rivers" probably from the foothills of the Zagros Mountains where he lived in caves and foraged for the small animals, wild fruits, and natural plants on which he subsisted. Then, at

some point, probably about 10,000 B.C., he learned gradually, largely by chance and happenstance, to plant and
harvest edible crops. He domesticated the wild ass, goat,
and sheep. And he learned to build huts of mud, for there
was no other building material in the area, and eventually
to bind the mud together with straw. None of this was
done quickly. Man's change from nomadism evolved
slowly and painfully over centuries, many centuries.

Man, beginning with the family and the tribe, eventually
evolved the village and then the city, and later learned to
wall the city in, as a protection from his enemies, both animal and human. One of the earliest of the serious excavations came in the late nineteenth century at a site some two
hundred miles north of the Persian Gulf to unearth the
ancient Sumerian city of Ur—the Ur of the Chaldees in
the Bible, from where Abraham, the father of three religions, began his journey into Canaan. Digging continued
at Ur well into the twentieth century, tracing the first
habitation there back some three thousand years.

Then, in 1948, excavations were carried out at Jarmo, a
village in the foothills of the Zagros in what is now Kurdistan. There archaeologists peeled back layer after layer of
ancient habitation, discovering that the people in the
earliest (of fifteen levels) dated back some six thousand
years and were too primitive to make earthenware, but
advanced enough to build huts of several rooms, make
stone axes and jewelry, and also to raise varieties of wheat,
barley, peas, and beans.

There have been, of course, dozens of other "digs,"
many of them of great interest and importance—Eridu, a

few miles to the south of Ur; Uruk, where it was necessary to go down seventy feet to reach virgin soil and where, eighteen layers down, was discovered the original village of Kullab, about four thousand years old; and Halaf and Obeid and others. And, of course, probably the oldest of them all, the Biblical city of Jericho.

The Wilderness of Judea, that comparatively tiny stretch of desert from the Judean Mountains to the Dead Sea and part of modern Israel, is a land of arid soil through which naked rocks thrust in monotonous confusion, a hot, dry land that has attracted as many odd bits of romantic history as any place in the Middle East. David fled there as a shepherd to escape the wrath of Saul and again (probably) when his son Absalom revolted against his rule. Solomon, in one of his lovelier compositions, sang of the beauties of the vineyards of 'En Gedi, a Judean Wilderness oasis. And in another of its oases, near the north end of the Dead Sea, was the walled city of Jericho. Actually there have been three Jerichos, the Old Testament Jericho, the New Testament Jericho, and today's existing Jericho, all in the same area, all products of the same spring-watered oasis.

It is the most ancient Jericho which Joshua, in the course of his incredibly bloodthirsty campaign to regain the Palestinean homeland of the Tribes of Israel, marched his army round and round until on the seventh day "the walls came tumbling down" and the two thousand or so residents were put to the sword.

The excavations in old Jericho were carried out between 1952 and 1958, and uncovered a series of habitations reaching well back before ceramics were in use, dated through the use of carbon 14 as a measuring method on charcoal and bone, to before 8,000 B.C. While the archaeologists were surprised at the antiquity of the walled city a thousand feet below sea level, they were more impressed at its size: some hundred or more acres in area and some two thousand in living inhabitants. That figure, by the way, was arrived at by the number of grindstones, mortars, and pestles found in the ruins, indicative of food produced and eaten.

Between the first settlement of villages like Jarmo and cities like Jericho and the beginnings of recorded history, time is compressed, literally. Many centuries passed before anything of importance occurred; that is, the centuries between the mortar and pestle to grind the first home-grown grains and the time when the first cuneiform tablet was inscribed or the first ziggurat built by pagan worshipers. The earliest settlers in the silted levees of the Tigris and the Euphrates were the Ubadians, whose origin is not clear but who grew into enterprising farmers and who, over the centuries, dotted the plains of southern Mesopotamia with their farms and villages, their canals and irrigation systems, and probably their small herds.

Their efficiency and prosperity also ordained their fate, for success breeds envy and invites takeover. Somewhere around 4,000 B.C., nomadic tribes from Syria in one direction and the Arabian Peninsula in another—both of Semitic cast—began to invade the Ubadian settlements, sometimes as immigrants, more often as conquerors. The meld of these early peoples was completed with the arrival

MESOPOTAMIA

of the Sumerians, some five centuries later: 3,500 B.C. These, the Sumerians, built the first true civilization known, one of many complex achievements and one which set the course of human behavior and culture on the path which has led to the present, for better or for worse as you may judge it.

The remarkable Sumerians invented the wheel and its accompanying rotary shaft (thus making possible the chariot, among other vehicles), learned to apply heat to metal and to create hundreds of durable tools, including both cooking utensils and the tools of war: spears and swords. They went further and applied the heating process to the manufacture of bricks and pottery.

The Sumerians invented writing. They also devised a

standard system of weights and measure and timekeeping—the 360-degree circle, the twenty-four hour day, the sixty-minute hour—the sailing vessel, the epic poem, and the proverb: ("Flatter a young man and he will give you anything." "Conceiving is fun, pregnancy tedious.").

The government of the early communities of the Sumerians was democratic, as the Ubadian had been. The individuals of any group, though probably only the males at that time, simply met when faced with a decision and adopted a course of action by common consent. As life became more complex, however, it was inevitable that rivalries would come up, disputes over land and water rights occur, and inevitable also that at some point the settlement was by force. Warfare at any level was not something that could be handled satisfactorily by community decision, so—and again the course of inevitability—the wisest or strongest, and more likely the latter, was elected to lead. And with success, to retain leadership and to assume certain prerogatives with it. And thus, kingship was born and in some form or other has been with the world ever since, along with the rivalries and wars.

Today's world of archaeology knows a great deal about the Sumerians from the excavations at Ur and Kish and a dozen other Mesopotamian cities. They built their homes around open inner courts and the outer walls were windowless, with low doors opening on narrow streets. Into these streets they dumped garbage and other refuse which piled up, stank, and bred rats. The temples and many of the better homes had amazingly well-equipped kitchens with fireplaces for some types of cooking and flat-topped ranges for other, brick tables, the working surface of which had been covered with a type of asphalt, and domed ovens for baking bread. There were wells in many of the kitchens or courtyards, though the poorer homes usually made do with a community well.

Several Sumerian cities carried out important trading activities with the caravans of the day, and Ur was particularly notable as a Persian Gulf port to which were brought goods from Egypt, Ethiopia, and the lands of the Far East: gold, copper, tin, ivory, various hard woods and stone which had been used for ballast, spices, and silk. Each city had a public square with public grounds where there were wrestling matches, gambling games, reciting poets, singers, and storytellers; taverns for the roisterers and bazaars for shoppers. These latter were much as they are in Middle Eastern cities today—narrow passages either above or underground, filled with scores of small booths.

The society of the day was divided into three distinct classes: the aristocracy, the commoner who comprised the bulk of the populace, and the slave. The wealth of the aristocracy usually derived from large landholdings, although the aristocrat might also be a military general or a high priest. The commoner, as usual, provided the bulk of the skills which made the civilization possible. He was the farmer, the carpenter, the scribe, the cattle breeder, the hunter and fisherman, smith, carpenter, and brickmaker. The slaves, who frequently held fairly high positions in the households of the wealthy, were sometimes prisoners of war and sometimes simply had been sold into slavery as children to escape extreme poverty. Entire families occasionally so sold themselves.

Barley was the staple food of the day, baked into bread or made into porridge (and also brewed into a very potent beer). Other grains were grown and eaten, of course, including several varieties of wheat. Fish was frequently on the table, chiefly carp and eel from the marshlands, which also contributed wildfowl. And the herds provided lamb, mutton, goat, and beef.

Like other men and women of that time, the Sumerians were unable to explain many of the natural phenomenon of life: the evils of drought, pestilence, storms, floods—or the benevolence of good weather which brought good harvests, the fertility of wives and livestock, victory in warfare.

So they invented gods and put them in charge of these unexplainable phenomena and learned to worship and propitiate (and sometimes curse) them. Since the gods had to have a place to live and since they were generally invisible—except on those rare occasions when they chose to show themselves—man tended to give them abodes that he, himself, couldn't reach: the remotest of mountain tops or the unreachable sky itself. And, in order to worship these on high, it seemed logical that the nearer one could get the more likely the message to be received. Thus came the ziggurats, which began as simple mud platforms designed for worship, and developed into temples of brick and stone which grew high and higher, serving first families, then clans, and finally entire communities. One such was the Biblical Tower of Babel, built on the Shinar plains of Babylonia, according to Genesis. The ziggurats, incidentally, long predated the pyramids and did not serve as burial places, although tombs were frequently placed right next door, so to speak. While the gods of the ziggurats provided spiritual comfort for the residents of the city and looked after their safety and well-being, the actual carrying out of these chores was entrusted to a king, at first elected but later hereditary. In addition to leading his nations' forces in time of war, the king was also responsible for keeping up roads, water conduits, irrigation systems and other public works. He had to keep the old temples in repair and build newer and better ones if he was to retain the respect of the gods (and the worshipers). He also was responsible for protection of the weak and for maintaining law and order. As early as 2500 B.C., Mesopotamians were living by a legal code and executing contracts, deeds of sale, and other commercial documents, all recorded on clay tablets in cuneiform lettering.

Burial grounds which have been unearthed contained many of the personal possessions of the dead and also reveal much about their habits of dress. Bodies were normally placed on the side for burial, in a sleeping position with a cup held to the mouth. In the tombs of the wealthy or of royalty, the cup was gold and the graves contained personal belongings obviously treasured and used by the deceased—silver helmets, belts, buckles, and rings for the men; necklaces, bracelets, anklets, combs, vanities, and elaborate gowns and headdresses of gold for the women. Frequently, also, graves alongside contained chariots which had been driven there, and the remains of servants, both in place presumably to serve in the next life.

The history of the Sumerians is one of almost continual combat of city-state against city-state until one, Kish, whose excavated ruins lie some fifty miles south of today's Baghdad, established sovereignty over the whole country about 3000 B.C. During the next millennium, it traded supremacy with Erech, which had been built a hundred or so miles to the southeast of Kish, with Lagash (thirty-five miles northeast of Erech), and with Ur, nearer the Persian Gulf. It also submitted briefly to the rule of the Semitic Akkadians.

The Sumerians, all in all, retained control over Mesopotamia for nearly twelve hundred years. Their political destruction began with the conquest and destruction of Ur, about 2000 B.C. and was ended completely by 1850 B.C.

CHAPTER VI

The Egyptians

WHILE Mesopotamia was establishing its heritage as the "Cradle of Civilization," another and parallel civilization was born, developed, and thrived in Egypt. There the river Nile was to the Egyptians, in far greater degree, what the Tigris and the Euphrates were to the Ubadians, the Sumerians, and the later peoples who lived in the more northern valley.

From the Mountain of the Moon in Ethiopia, the Blue Nile flows to Khartoum in the Sudan, where it is joined by the White Nile and the two course four thousand miles to the famous Egyptian Delta on the Mediterranean. As the Nile travels north from the junction at Khartoum, it is interrupted six times by cataracts. Numbered from mouth to source, the first cataract is at Aswan where the river enters Egypt, the sixth just below Khartoum. From Aswan, the Nile flows as an uninterrupted ribbon until it reaches the Delta, roughly a hundred miles from the sea, and there it fans out in tributaries over miles of mud flats.

The Nile Valley from Aswan, now the site of the Aswan Dam, has provided Egypt historically with about 13,000 square miles of rich cultivatible land. Lower Egypt—the area from Memphis, just above modern Cairo to the sea—lies within the reach of Mediterranean rains. Cairo near the top of the Delta will receive from one to two inches of rain annually. In Upper Egypt, from Memphis to Aswan, a year may pass with no rain at all—and often does.

Each year, as it has since time immeasurable, the Nile swells with the torrential rains which fall in the mountains of Ethiopia, flows north and spreads over Egypt in a bountiful flood. The earliest Egyptians were content to use the Nile waters as they rose and fell, leaving the rich alluvial deposit behind. At some later period they trapped the overflow behind dikes, holding it to soak the enclosed land. Then later they learned to build canals and reservoirs to conserve the water so that it could be used at any time during the year.

The Valley of the Nile in Upper Egypt spreads in width to twenty-five miles in some places, and shrinks to a single mile in others, all of it, of course, hugging the banks of the stream. The Delta, so named by the Greeks for its similarity in shape to the fourth letter of their alphabet, sits like an enormous slice of pie, its point at Memphis and widening out to the seacoast, an area about 125 miles from tip to the coast, north and south, and covering some fourteen hundred square miles.

The Nile historically has been completely responsible for the economy of Egypt; actually, the Nile *is* Egypt, in the sense that without the river there could have been no life and no nation.

Man probably settled the Valley of the Nile about the same time he found his way down to the "Land Between the Rivers," some ten or twelve thousand years ago, but his progress toward civilization was slower and it is probable that he did not begin to group into permanent settlements until about 4,000 B.C. Protected by deserts on the east and west which made military invasion virtually impossible, by the Mediterranean which was easily defendable on the north, and even by the cataracts of the Nile to the south, Egypt lived an isolated life. Whereas the plains of the Tigris and Euphrates were an open invitation to any marauding horde, Egypt lived for centuries at a time with never a threat of outside force.

While this gave the Egyptians security, it also inhibited new thoughts and ideas, and the Egyptians were nearly a millenium behind the Sumerians in some achievements. The scholars of Egypt never got around to devising a system of writing and calculating. They simply waited until the Sumerian systems filtered in via the trading caravans. Then they took Sumerian writing and calculating systems and adopted and improved them. They had never used the wheel until they were violently exposed to it (via chariots) during one of their infrequent invasions. Then they adopted it by necessity, and on a grander scale. They also learned about metal armor and weapons from the same invaders, and possibly about the fusing of the metals themselves.

As stonecutters, however, they had no equals or even competent copiers in that age. They originated the science of medicine and progressed far ahead of their era. And they devised a religious practice in which much of the current life was devoted tranquilly to preparing for death and the better life which would follow and which would be eternal. Egyptians have been pictured as being preoccupied with the expectation of death, gloomy and sad. They were not. They left voluminous records on the papyrus paper they invented and exported over the then known world, and many of the picture stories of Egyptian life portrayed were as informative as today's comic strips. They showed games of all kinds, jokes and pranks, occasional quarrels (two girls in a hair-pulling match), and all with comment, much of which was good-humored raillery. Why not? Death was not a sad affair when you had every reason to believe in a much better life thereafter. Osiris, who had been born mortal, slain and then restored to life, and who was obviously a compassionate being, was the King and Judge of the Underworld. As recounted in the *Book of the Dead*, a translation of Egyptian burial sermons, beliefs, and customs, judgment of the dead was held in the Court of Osiris. Those condemned (a very small percentage) were devoured by the Eater of the Dead and ceased to exist, while all others entered the domains of Osiris and found everlasting life and happiness.

There was no allusion to resurrection or eternal punishment. And no singing choirs of angels. People simply lived normal lives in the hereafter, eating, drinking, amusing themselves, all happily.

The society of ancient Egypt was divided into several classes. At the top, of course, was the Pharaoh. Originally, he was only king, but later became divine and hence a god. He was responsible, literally, for all things Egyptian: the rise and fall of the Nile, the success or failure of the harvests, victory or defeat in warfare. Under the Pharaoh was a small class of nobles, then came civil officials, thou-

sands of scribes who kept tally on everything for the records and for tax purposes, a small class of artisans, usually
those skilled in the art of stonecutting and building, then
the millions of common laborers. The Pharaoh lived as he
wished, usually quite well, indeed. The nobles lived lavishly on great estates with servants outdoor and in, many
of whom were slaves bought in the open markets. The
scribes and artisans led respected lives; their skills were
essential. And the commoner was not really so badly off
most of the time. True, he could be conscripted for just
about anything, usually for pyramid or other memorial
building, but that was only for three months a year, normally, during the flood season when he couldn't work in
the fields. Also, this was a labor of love for the gods and
presumably enhanced his chances for immortality. The
rest of the time he tilled his land which, by title, belonged to the Pharaoh (who theoretically owned the entire
country) but which the peasant inherited, bought, sold,
and paid taxes on.

The chronological history of Egypt, century by century,
dynasty by dynasty, is fascinating, timeless, and intermin-
able. In the earliest of days Egypt was divided into small
kingdoms grouped as Lower Egypt (the Delta) and Upper
Egypt, from Memphis to the first cataract at Aswan.
These two areas, along with their city-states were unified
by Menes around 3000 B.C. Menes was the first Pharaoh
to wear the double crown for both areas.

The 350 years which followed Menes saw some eighteen
successive Pharaohs solidify the national unity he had
begun through two dynasties, i.e., rulers of the same fam-

ily line. The third through eighth dynasties lasted through five hundred years of peace and prosperity and the period is known as the Age of the Pyramids, for it was during this time that the pryamids were built, first at Memphis for Djoser, the first Pharaoh of the Third Dynasty, then at Giza for Khufu (or Cheops, in Greek), near modern Cairo, and for Khafre and Menkaure, all of the Fourth Dynasty. Eighty that were built remain today.

Through successive centuries and dynasties which followed, Egypt was both up and down. Her armies conquered neighbors, including Palestine and Syria, and were conquered by invaders in turn. The Nubians, Assyrians, and Persians all took whacks at ruling Egypt until Alexander invaded in 322 B.C., kicked out the Persians, built the city of Alexandria and placed his lieutenant, Ptolemy, firmly on the throne. Ptolemy established a dynasty which lasted almost three hundred years—until Cleopatra, the last of the Ptolemy line, pressed an asp to her bosom in 30 B.C., after putting her money (and future) on the wrong Roman general.

With conquest by Augustus, Egypt now became a satellite of Rome, was Christianized to a degree, and then became a battleground for Muslim Arabs who swept over the entire Middle East in the seventh century. The Arabs controlled Egypt for nine centuries, to be succeeded by the Turks and then by the British after World War I. It was almost mid-twentieth century before Egypt finally became totally independent again.

CHAPTER **VII**

The Ten Conquerors

ALTHOUGH Sumer ceased to exist shortly after 2000 B.C., the influence of the Sumerian culture, technocratic achievements, and even religion continued for centuries. The conquering peoples who followed simply assimilated the Sumerians plus all their attainments—gods, language, arts, and sciences. Under some of the succeeding rules the culture retrogressed, but in the main, the following empires built on the Sumerian techniques and progress of civilization continued.

The kingdoms and dynasties and conquering forces which followed the Sumerians in the Middle East (some of them overlap) were:

—The Babylonians (1900-700 B.C.). The ultimate conquerors of Sumer were the Amorites, Semitic tribes of uncertain origin from Syria to the north and Arabia to the south. They had for years infiltrated Sumer as peaceful herdsmen, and they simply picked their moment to organize and take over. A local chieftain chose the then unimportant settlement of Babylon to be his headquarters and, within a few years, his successors had founded an Amorite dynasty, built his adopted town into a city of fabulous wealth and accoutrements, and eventually presented the name Babylonia to what had once been Sumer.

Most of this came about under King Hammurabi, who inherited a kingdom of a few hundred square miles and, at his death forty-two years later, controlled an empire of city-states he had conquered and which ranged from the Persian Gulf to modern Turkey and beyond. Hammurabi was wily, daring, and unscrupulous. He made treaties and broke them, bribed, beguiled, divided his enemies and destroyed them, one by one. Hammurabi is equally famous for his Code of Laws, believed to be the world's oldest, a copy of which, engraved on a stone stele, is in the Louvre of Paris. Along about 1600 B.C., the Kassites, non-Semitic tribes from the Zagros Mountains, conquered the descendants of Hammurabi, settled in, adopted the Babylonian language, gods, and customs—in fact, became more Babylonian than the Babylonians—and ruled for four hundred years, until defeated by the Assyrians.

—The Assyrians (950-600). The Assyrians, who achieved the dubious distinction of being rated as the cruelest of all the warring hordes of the day, had been building up to a conquest of the Middle East for centuries and reached the peak of their power during the seventh century before Christ. They constructed their own magnificent capital of Ninevah as a substitute for Babylon, which they destroyed after overrunning the nation in war. Assyrian King Sennacherib boasted that he filled the city of Babylon with corpses, leveled the buildings, burned and then flooded the ruins. He was later murdered by his own sons and succeeded by one of them, Essarhaddon, who rebuilt Babylon and then moved on to conquer Egypt, which had grown old and tired and offered little resistance. This conquest consolidated an empire which included Palestine and Syria, and stretched from the Aswan cataract to the borders of Armenia.

The Assyrians in their turn, of course, fell too, first to King Nebuchadnezzar in 605 B.C., who led a combined force of Medes and Chaldeans, and then to King Cyrus of Persia, now Iran. The latter added Babylonia to an already extensive empire by ousting Nebuchadnezzar, who had razed Jerusalem in 586 B.C., burned the Temple of Solomon, and exiled the Jews.

—The Kingdom of Judah (1000-550 B.C.). The Kingdom of Judah, later the Kingdom of Israel, paralleled much of the Assyrian reign in Mesopotamia. It was relatively unimportant in terms of military conquest or even great cultural achievements. From the standpoint of religion, however, it was vastly significant: it established for the first time the belief of monotheism, the supremacy of one God and only one.

Abraham, the father figure of both the Christian and Muslim religions, left the Sumerian city of Ur about 1900 B.C. and migrated north and westward, halting somewhere on the Syria-Palestine border. From Abraham and his two sons, Isaac and Ishmael, were descended today's Arabs (probably) and the Tribes of Israel. At some point—two, three, or even four hundred years later—Isaac's descendants and their families migrated to Egypt to escape famine and drought. They lived there in peace for generations but later found themselves intolerably persecuted by a new dynasty of Pharaohs and eventually followed Moses about 1000 B.C. by a circuitous route which eventually took them to Canaan, a land later called Palestine for the Philistines, and what is now, roughly, modern Israel.

There the campaigns of Joshua either exterminated or subjugated the Canaanites, and the Hebrews found the land fertile and productive. They originally lived as separate tribes until united by Saul and his son-in-law and successor, David, who had established himself by winning the one-on-one match against Goliath. David was followed by his son, Solomon the Wise, under whose rule the country prospered. After Solomon's death, however, the country divided in two sections with the two capitals, Israel in the north, with its capital of Samaria (from whence the origin of Good Samaritan), and Jerusalem of Judah in the south. In 721 B.C., Israel fell to the Assyrians and the often-called "Lost Tribes of Israel" were scattered throughout the Middle East. In 586 B.C., Judah was overrun by Nebuchadnezzar and the people of Judah again divided, some staying in Judah under Babylonian rule but the majority—who had now acquired the name "Jews" (from Judah)—took their books and records and belief in monotheism with them and returned to Babylon proper. It was twenty-five hundred years before they returned in numbers to what they had learned to call the homeland.

—The Persians (530-330 B.C.). In 530 B.C., King Cyrus brought his Persian troops out of their protected seclusion behind the Zagros Mountains and took over Mesopotamia—the territory the Medes had wrested from the

Assyrians and additional territory they had not. Cyrus was a kindly ruler (for his time) who tried tolerance and persuasion. His successors, Kings Darius I and Xerxes, were more inclined to force and pushed the empire across Turkey and to the borders of Greece. Xerxes died in 465 B.C. and with him died also the Persian will for further conquest. The Persian rule of Babylonia ended in 334 B.C. when Alexander the Great conquered Mesopotamia and Persia and peacefully occupied Egypt.

—Alexander the Great (330 B.C.-A.D. 64). Alexander swept out of Greece in 330 B.C., pushed the Persians back to their mountain plateau, and in eleven years forged an empire larger than any before known—all of Macedonia, Egypt, and far into India. More important, he and the successors he left on various thrones, made serious efforts to both educate the conquered peoples about Greek culture, language, and customs, and to convert them to it, a process known as "Hellenization," stemming, of course, from the word "Hellenes," meaning "Greeks." It was the first serious attempt at an interchange of Western and Eastern cultures.

—The Roman Empire (30 B.C.-A.D. 570). Moving from antiquity into the days of the Roman Empire seems almost like moving into modern history. By Julius Caesar's time, Rome was already busily picking apart the remains of Alexander's empire and frequently meddling imperiously into the affairs of Egypt. When Caesar marched his troops into Alexandria in the first century B.C., Cleopatra, last of the Ptolemys, became his mistress. She quickly switched over to Anthony after Caesar's assassination, and when he was defeated by Augustus at Actium and committed suicide, Cleopatra followed suit rather than be taken to Rome as a prisoner. That was the year 30 B.C.

Rome, which was busily building its empire, was not interested in the whole of the Middle East (the vast desert lands were useless to them) and consequently occupied themselves with the "Fertile Crescent" and Egypt. During the years Rome controlled this much of the Middle East, Jesus was born in the Palestinian town of Bethlehem, and with Him, Christianity.

The followers of Christ were, of course, persecuted for years, but by the fourth century Christianity had been accepted as the official religion. In A.D. 312 Emperor Constantine moved the capital of the Roman Empire to Byzantium and renamed it Constantinople. (It is now Istanbul, on the European side of Turkey and the Bosphorus). There the cultures of the Greek, Christian, and Middle East blended and borrowed from each other until the rise of Islam.

—Islam (570-1300). Muhammad was born in Mecca, on the Arabian Peninsula, about 570 and, by the time of his death in 632, had firmly established the Islamic religion and gained military control of the entire Arabian Peninsula. In the century following his death, the Islamic Arabs pushed westward across North Africa, into Spain and southern France, not to be halted until the Battle of Tours in 732. Under Islam the Middle East flourished. A new city, and for a time, the capital, was built at Damascus in Syria. Mecca and Medina were rebuilt; Baghdad became a center of study of philosophy, the arts, and sciences. And Harun al-Rashid, a caliph of the Abbassid Dynasty who reigned from 786 to 809, became famous in literature as the caliph of Scheherazade's "One Thousand and One Nights."

Then, in the eleventh century, Islam was taken over by a horde of new and fervid converts, the Seljuk Turks. They were Mongol-related nomads from Central Asia and they brought with them an inherited militancy and a hatred of things European. The Turks had permitted pilgrims of all religions to visit the shrines of Jerusalem. The Seljuks decreed the city was only for Muslims. The result was the Crusades.

—The Crusades (1099-1272). There were eight crusades in all. The first, in 1099, was made by Western European Christians with the intent of restoring Christian rule. Most of the succeeding Crusades were made largely with the intent of reinforcing the first and seizing control of the major Islamic ports and, probably, providing an outlet for the more adventurous males of the period, some motivated by religious fervor, others with the gleam of treasure in their eyes.

The early Crusaders took over Nazareth, the boyhood home of Jesus, made it the religious and political center of Galilee, in the far north of Palestine, and held it for two centuries. They dominated several small states on the eastern Mediterranean, colonized the areas, and intermarried with local ladies of Christian faith. They greatly increased the trade between the Mediterranean ports, and with Europe, and when the Mamluks, the fierce Muslims of Egypt, gradually gained control with the last battle at Acre in 1291, the victors were content to let the Christian merchants remain and conduct business.

—The Ottoman Empire (1450-1918). In the thirteenth century a second wave of Mongol nomads filtered into Turkey, were converted to Islam, and adapted into such an efficient military force that they eventually took over from the Seljuk Turks who were in control of most of the Middle East. They took the name Ottoman from their leader and rapidly earned the respect of the rest of Islam by driving the last of the Byzantine forces out of Asia Minor, and pushing into southeastern Europe. Here, by 1400, they controlled much of the Balkan Peninsula and had taken over Constantinople which they renamed Istanbul, as their capital. Under Suleiman the Magnificent, who ruled from 1520 to 1566, the Ottoman Empire reached from Algeria to Persia, its only rival in the Eastern world.

After Suleiman's death, the Ottoman Empire began a slow but certain decline until eventually it became known throughout Europe and in Russia as the "Sick Man of Europe," an illness the other powers hoped fervently would be nothing less than fatal. The Ottoman slippage coincided with the rise of the European nations, which were going through the last of the Renaissance and the beginning of the Industrial Age. The Ottoman rulers were forced by one pressure or another into acquiescing to the digging of the Suez Canal in 1869, along with making many other concessions in banking and commerce, until by the end of the nineteenth century France, Britain, Russia, Italy, and Austria virtually controlled the economy of the Ottoman Empire. Russia had dominion over the north end of the Black Sea, along with naval rights on that entire body of water, plus access through the Bosphorus to the Mediterranean. Most of the Balkan nations had regained their independence or had drifted under the control of Great Britain and France. The French had annexed North Africa; the British dominated Egypt, as well as southern Persia. Only the lands of the "Fertile Crescent" remained in Ottoman hands, along with European and Asian Turkey. Then, in 1914, Turkey joined Germany in World War I and in the dividing-up process which followed, the Ottoman Empire was confined to Turkey and Turkey alone. Only Mustafa Kemal, also called Ataturk, who emerged as the strong man after the division, prevented its total dismemberment. He abolished the remnants of the Ottoman Empire (along with the veil for Turkish women), moved the capital from Istanbul to Ankara, and brought Turkey into the modern world.

—After World War I. To gain needed support, the Allies had made many promises to the countries of the Middle East, some of them mutually contradictory, and when the time came for settlement after the Armistice there were many bitter disillusionments; the Arabs have long memories of that, reaching to the present.

The Arabs on the Peninsula had, at British urging and under the leadership of the legendary Lawrence of Arabia, revolted against the Ottoman rule. The promised reward was an independent state to include the "Fertile Crescent." When the last papers were signed in faraway Paris, however, Arabia found itself confined to the Peninsula and not all of that. Ibn Sa'ud, who had established the rule of the House of Sa'ud in 1902, became the first king of the country he had consolidated in 1932 and changed its name to Saudi Arabia. Although Ibn Sa'ud was an absolute (also wise and just) monarch, he had to tolerate almost incessant interference in the affairs of the country by England and France, until it finally gained real independence after World War II.

Egypt had been a British protectorate since 1914 and continued to be one until the late 1940s when the British finally and reluctantly withdrew.

The nations of the "Fertile Crescent" were responsible for a new international political term—the mandate. Syria, Lebanon, Iraq, Jordan, and Palestine were made mandates of the League of Nations, which in turn mandated them to the control of the British and the French. Britain got Iraq, Palestine, and Jordan. The French took Lebanon and Syria. All finally became independent after World War II.

Iran, once fabled Persia, had been a military and political testing ground for Britain and Russia since 1907, divided into a Russian zone on the north, a neutral zone in the center, and a British zone in the south. During the

first World War the Russians and British joined sides to
fight the Ottoman forces. From the resulting chaos a rebel
leader, Reza Kahn, arose to overthrow the government
of the Persian Shah in 1921 and eventually drove out both
the Russians and the British. The old Shah abdicated and
Reza Kahn was named to that post in 1925. Iran has been
independent since.

The settlement of the Jews in Palestine began in 1923
as an implementation of the Balfour Declaration. James
Arthur Balfour, then Foreign Secretary of England and
later noted for his devotion to the cause of international
peace, issued the Balfour Declaration in 1917 in order to
gain the support of influential Jews throughout the world.
It pledged Britain's support for a Jewish national homeland in Palestine. The result of the 1923 action was immediate protests from the Arabs, which grew in force and
violence after Hitler's Jewish persecutions in Germany
saw more and more Jews fleeing Europe to the ancient
homeland. After World War II, the United Nations partitioned Palestine into two states, one Jewish and one
Arab, with Jerusalem an open, international city. The
result has been almost constant border hostilities since,
and four major armed conflicts.

CHAPTER **VIII**

The People

From the beginning of history, the Middle East has both benefited and suffered from wave after wave of immigration, some of it peaceful but more often not. Probably no region has a more heterogeneous population, with physical characteristics from almost every part of the earth—black, olive, and white. There is virtually no purity of race, but in contrast to this, a great number of distinct groups have maintained a mosaic of identities, through religion, dress, customs, professions, language dialects, and simply by like clinging to like, even in the thronged cities.

To achieve an understanding of the peoples of the Middle East—and it is a terribly complex situation—it is reasonable to approach the problem from three directions: racially, occupationally, and geographically, each separately and in turn.

Racially, the Middle East population divides into three major groups: Semitic, that is, Arabs and Jews; Iranian or Persian; and Turkish.

The Semites are by far the largest of the classifications, well over a hundred million, and also the most confusing. According to the Old Testament, which both Jew and Muslim accepts, the Patriarch Abraham's first born, of wife Hagar, was Ishmael. His second son, by wife Sarah, was Isaac. Ishmael migrated south and married an Egyptian woman who bore him twelve sons. Arabic tradition today holds that present-day Arabs are descendants of these twelve sons.

Meanwhile, Isaac remained with Abraham. He also married and fathered many sons and became the leader of the Hebrews who settled in Canaan, now Israel. They were, of course, the first people to claim the supremacy of a single god, and modern Judaism traces itself to this beginning.

It has been said that the only reliable identification of an Arab is that a man is an Arab if he says he is. This same expression has also been applied to the Jew. Neither term (Jew or Arab) is racial, nor does either define a single national entity. Arab states are frequently hostile to each other and have never maintained a unity for long, and Jews are too widely scattered over the earth to be yet a firm nationality. Most Arabs are Muslims, but some are of Jewish faith and several million are Christian. Most Arabs speak Arabic in one dialect or another, but several million other Middle Easterners who are not Arabs also speak Arabic, including thousands of Jews. Jews in Israel speak many different languages. Besides Father Abraham and the Hebrews, the Arabs and Jews have other common Semitic ancestors: the Akkadians, Assyrians, Canaanites, and Phoenicians. (Of these ancient tribes or peoples, only the Hebrews today retain an identity.)

The Turks of today, second numerically, show little relationship to their ancestors, nomads from the steppes of Central Asia, who were predominantly Mongols but

had a mixing of the Caucasian. With the fall of the Ottoman Empire and its division after World War I, Kemal
Ataturk successfully expelled both the European conquerors and the ancient Empire rulers from Turkey
proper, and embarked on a program to modernize (and
Westernize) the country. He banned the teaching of religion in schools (the people are predominantly Muslim),
took Turkish women out from behind their veils, replaced the Arabic script with Latin characters, and replaced the Ottoman laws with the Western code. It was a
remarkable process. When Turkey joined NATO after
World War II, American Air Force instructors found, in
teaching some of the young men from mountain villages,
that they were moving from the oxen to the aircraft, by-
passing not only the motor car but the wagon and the
cart; some of the boys out of the mountain fastnesses had
never seen a wheel and before they could learn about a
doorknob, they first had to have the door explained.
Neither of these things kept them from becoming first-rate
airmen.

The Iranians, once Persians—whose history is as glamorous in literature as it is varied in real life—were probably a mixed bag originally, migrants from Eastern
Europe and Central Asia. They, like the Turks, are non-
Semitic; in fact, the name "Iran" is vaguely related to the
term "Aryan." About three-fourths of the nation's population of thirty-two million are Iranian and the remainder
Kurds and Turks. The language is related to neither
Arabic nor Turkish, but leans more to the European
tongues.

In addition to the three large population groups mentioned above, there are several minorities in the Middle East: Europeans (including Russians), North and South Americans, and East and South Africans. Since the early 1930s, when oil began to play an increasingly large part in world finance and politics, some of the minorities have increased considerably, especially the French, German, British, North and South Americans, and Russians.

Occupationally, Middle Easterners fall readily into three major categories: the nomad, the villager, and the city dweller. (Within these three divisions there are a score or more subdivisions, largely based on geography. These will come later.)

The true nomads of the Middle East were once powerful, warring tribes who competed with central authority and often were the real control in many areas. Today they are a vanishing breed, reduced in number by mechanized central government forces with modern armament, by intermural warfare, and probably more than anything— by evolution. When the motorized wheel arrived (and the airplane), the camel ceased to be the only means of travel over the desert. The raising, buying, and selling of camels, their hair, hides, milk, and meat has provided a means of livelihood for the nomad for thousands of years. When the demand for the camel goes, so must the nomad.

The life of the nomad is either romantic or dreadful, depending on the viewpoint. The nomad leads a free life; he is burdened with few rules, he has no office and no office hours, no traffic problems, no air pollution; his home is the desert or the mountains, with, quite literally, the sun in the morning and the stars at night. On the other hand, he has no running water, no electricity, no furniture, few doctors or dentists, and his diet and personal living habits would appall most people of the Western world.

The desert nomad lives in a black tent made of camel hair, and the size of the tent and its number of poles depends on the state of his wealth. There is, usually, one tent to a family, divided in the center with one side for the male adults and the other for the women and small children. The tent is pitched, quite naturally, so that the opening is to the leeward. Over the entrance is an awning and here the males of the family, and frequently male visitors, gather to drink the obligatory three cups of coffee. (Visitors never see the feminine members.) Within the tent are rugs and mats for the floor, cooking utensils, and the few clothes the family affords.

Winter is the time of desert rains and these produce spots of green throughout the desert which serve as camping sites as long as the forage lasts. In the summer, desert nomads move to an oasis, where the tribe may actually own land or may only camp there. Here they sell the products of the winter—mats, blankets, and articles of clothing woven from the hair of their animals—sell and trade camels, accumulate enough money to buy the things they must: mostly food. Their diet consists of the milk of the camel in some form—liquid, cheese, curds or butter; wheat and barley made into soups, meat rarely; dates or other dried fruits.

Other nomads vary their lives between the plains, often deserts, and the mountains, and in addition to camels, which they use for transport and beasts of burden, they also shepherd flocks of sheep and goats.

The rural village of the Middle East has varied little in the past twenty centuries. Except for sometimes a school or hospital bought with recent oil money, the village is much the same now as it was when Christ walked the streets of Nazareth. The residents are peasants, almost always farmers, and they tend to live in the same way of their fathers before them.

The village, usually two hundred people or a few more, is made up of families, each headed by the eldest male whose authority over the younger members ranges from total to how much he wishes to tolerate dissent. The family consists of sons and grandsons and their wives, the unmarried daughters and the children—from a dozen to half a hundred people. They live in an individual enclave, either one house or a group of houses built around a courtyard. Individual family units are small; one or two rooms are normal, three is luxury. And they are often shared with the farm animals. The houses are windowless, maybe one or two stories, and normally have a flat roof where the occupants often sleep in hot weather. One family complex is normally jammed against another, for the land is precious. Streets are narrow, winding haphazardly. Since interfamily marriage is encouraged, often entire villages will be related.

The residents of the village till the soil of the surrounding farms, ranging as far away as two miles, for that is

about as far as the farmer can afford the time to walk
twice daily. He raises mostly food crops and his farm will
rarely be larger than five acres, on which he grows barley,
wheat, corn, millet, and rice, any of which may be made
into bread, soups, or noodles. There will be a vegetable
garden for onions, cucumbers, beans, eggplant, tomatoes,
and peppers. Someone in the village will have a grove of
fruit trees: grapes, figs, apricots, peaches, and pomegran-
ates. Nuts are grown and also, of course, olives, to be
eaten raw or made into the indispensable oil for a dozen
uses. Dates are a major crop of the desert oases.

Cities in the Middle East have the same purpose they do
elsewhere in the world, that is, to serve the needs of an
area—commercial, religious, military, political, educa-
tional, cultural. Most of them are old, built in the early
centuries A.D., or even before. (Two exceptions are Port
Said, built along with the Suez Canal about 1860, and Tel
Aviv, Israel's largest city, founded in 1909.)

There are four cities in the Middle East of more than
a million population. Cairo (Egypt) is by far the largest
with three and a half million. Tehran (Iran) and Istanbul (Turkey) have about two million people each. And
Casablanca has nearly one and a quarter million. Algiers
(Algeria), Damascus (Syria), and Tunis (Tunisia) and
Baghdad (Iraq) are other leaders in the modern population field.

The cities of the Middle East today are cities of contrast, the very old with the very new. All of them have
been modernized to some extent, mostly by and for the

Europeans or those Middle Easterners who have been accustomed to Western air conditioning, plumbing, and telephones. Sometimes the modern city blends with the ancient; more often the modern sits alongside the old, almost entirely separate, although the Hilton Hotel and the Holiday Inn may be only a few blocks from the central Mosque and the old town bazaar.

The new cities of the Middle East are like modern cities in any part of Europe and America—skyscrapers, traffic jams, apartment dwelling, and even supermarkets, with a touch of the East, perhaps, but little more than a tur-banned doorman, a splashing fountain, or a minaret-topped structure looking slightly out of place.

The old city, however, can be endlessly fascinating—narrow streets, packed trolleys, a dozen forms of dress. The largest or most important mosque is usually also the city center, adjoining important government buildings or an ancient fortress where the Saracens held off the infidels (or didn't). From its minaret, the *muezzin* calls the faithful to prayer five times a day; its courtyard is a gathering place for discussion, gossip, and sometimes political exhortation. There is more than one mosque in the cities, of course. Probably the most beautiful in the Middle East is the Blue Mosque in Istanbul, where sunlight filtered through the window glass stained in various shades—but predominantly blue—shines on the rich oriental rugs which cover the floors, also in shades of blue.

Sometimes the old city's major bazaar, or *souk*, will be near the major mosque, sometimes not. In Istanbul the bazaar is in what once were the royal stables—miles of

underground passageways where you may buy almost anything transportable, jewelry to rug to bubble pipe, and
you must bargain earnestly with the merchant, for otherwise he will lose all respect for you.

Some of the ancient mystic of the craft guilds still lingers
in the Middle East, going back to the time when each
trade guarded the secrets of its craft jealously and was
organized tightly with secret rites and rituals of the guild
hall, admitting new members almost entirely on a father-
son basis. Frequently these guilds were so strong that they
occupied and ruled individual sections of the city. Even
today the Middle East city dweller feels a loyalty to his
own neighborhood leader rather than to the city as a
whole. This applies also to sections of the Middle East
cities which have partitioned themselves into religious or
ethnic groups: Christian, Jew, Armenian, Turkish.

This, however, is confined to the old city. In the new
part, occupied almost entirely by the well-to-do or upper
middle class—professional people, military officers, government officials, and foreign businessmen with their families—living is much like that in New York's upper Third
Avenue, Paris' Sixteenth *arrondissement,* or London's
West End.

CHAPTER IX

Mountains and Deserts

MAN is not necessarily the product of his environment but his manner of living is inevitably shaped by his interaction with his land and its climate. This is infinitely true of the Middle East.

In shape, this group of divergent countries which make up the Middle East is an irregular rectangle. From the Mediterranean Sea to the Indian Ocean it stretches five thousand miles and its greatest breadth is from the Black Sea to the Nile, some two thousand miles.

About four-fifths of the region between these boundaries is desert, dry and desolate, very hot by day and bitterly cold by night, and most of the rest is mountains, rugged and rarely enticing. The inhospitality of desert and mountains, however, is relieved by verdant river valleys, desert oases, and coastal areas where the great majority of the Middle Easterners are jammed on a small percentage of the land.

To identify the widely varying people of the Middle East with the land on which they live, and which dictates or at least strongly influences the way they live, it is helpful here also to consider the area in sectors—this time six, ranging from Turkey in Asia and Europe, to the Sahara Desert in North Africa.

*   *   *

Turkey, at the top of the map, has a narrow coastline ringed with mountains, the highest peak of which, at 17,000 feet, is Mount Ararat, which Noah made his first port of call after the flood. The mountains flatten out eventually into a series of wide plateaus, the most central of which is Anatolia. These plateaus are Turkey's major source of agricultural production.

Turkey has a population of almost forty million people, some 90 percent of whom live on the Asian side and the remainder across the Bosphorus in Europe. The capital of Turkey is Ankara, a city created to be the capital. The major population center is Istanbul, which, as Byzantium, had been the center of the Byzantine Empire and, as Constantinople for a time, the center of the Holy Roman Empire. Today it is a trade center and superlative tourist attraction. It is on the European side. Modern Turkey has nearly half its border with Europe and Russia, and inclines toward Europe culturally, commercially, and militarily.

The Turks are a vehemently independent people—hardy, fierce, and formidable opponents in any conflict. In addition to its own ethnic people, described earlier, Turkey also has a large minority of Armenians, most of them concentrated near the eastern border with Russia, across which in Soviet Armenia they also live in large numbers.

The Armenians are old-time inhabitants of Turkey, having established their own kingdom in the foothills of Mount Ararat in the early A.D. centuries. Throughout the years they were routinely subjugated and persecuted by one invader or another but managed to cling, as they still do, to their distinctive dress, blood lines, language, and the long-acquired habit, now legendary, of being the sharpest traders in the Middle East. They had to be to survive.

During World War I the Ottoman Turks, who had never really cared very much for the Armenian presence in their midst anyway, used the excuse of their possible collaboration with Russia to either export or exterminate a million and a half of them. Others, however, are widely scattered throughout the Middle East and, to some degree, the world.

Farthest eastward of all the Middle Eastern countries is Iran, long known as Persia, a land of purple nights and fabulous tales. Iran consists largely of a central plateau, averaging some four thousand feet in height. Two great mountain ranges tower over the plateau, the Zagros on the south and east, and the Elburz on the north. There are two coastal plains, one along the Caspian Sea on the Russian side and the other along the Persian Gulf and the Gulf of Oman across from the Arabian Peninsula. The center of the plateau is covered by the forbidding salt swamp called the Kavir. The vast area is covered with thick layers of salt, much of it broken and saw-toothed, which lie on top of a bog and seeping water. Understandably, much of the Kavir is unexplored.

Iran, which, as Persia, was a military power some twenty-five hundred years ago and which today is again powerful due to its vast oil fields, has a wide variety of people within its borders. The Persians, who are a tall people of lighter skin than many fellow-Middle Easterners, are the dominate group in Iran. Although they live in most parts of the country, the Persians are concentrated in the densely populated north from where they dominate the commerce and industry of the country from the urban areas and the agriculture from the rural. Although a dozen languages and dialects are spoken in Iran, the official language is Persian.

In the south and east, where Iran has borders with Afghanistan and Pakistan, Iran is peopled predominantly by the Baluchs. In their own homeland of Baluchistan, off the Gulf of Oman, the swarthy, bearded Baluchs wrest a meager living from the near-desert plains and the rough mountain slopes by herding camels, goats, and sheep. They are periodic nomads and in the past were aggressive fighters, raiding the towns and villages of the area. Stronger government policing has stopped this practice mostly, and some of the Baluchi males have turned to the oil field for living money. The womenfolk excel at weaving and needlecraft.

The "Fertile Crescent," formed from parts of Jordan, Syria, Israel, and Iraq, and shaped, as the name foretells, in the form of a crescent, is the heartland and birthplace of this ancient world of the Middle East. The area owes much of its fertility to the bounty of the Tigris and Euphrates rivers, which rise in the little Caucasus Mountains of Turkey, flow through Syria and Iraq, almost merge at Baghdad, finally do meet in the lowlands of Iraq, and then flow into the Persian Gulf. Israel may thank the Mediterranean climate of hot, dry summers and moderate, rainy winters for its productivity. Jordan, not so fortunate, still has sufficient rainfall for productive agriculture in a considerable part of the country.

Jordan, like so many other countries of the Middle East, has one major feature in its physical structure—a plateau rising to some twenty-five hundred feet. The upper parts of this, approximately 25 percent of the country, have an annual rainfall sufficient to support useful agriculture. Elsewhere the climate is hot and arid, and the people resort to pastoral nomadism, herding sheep, camels, goats, and cattle from green spot to green spot. The great majority of Jordan's population is Arabic, although they vary considerably in physical characteristics—the farmer, the urban dweller, and the nomad.

Syria can be divided into two major areas—the west where some 80 percent of the population lives and which receives forty to fifty inches of rain each year, and the much larger and relatively arid east.

Fronting the Mediterranean seacoast on the west rises the five thousand-foot Jebel Ansariyeh mountain ridge which slips gently into the sea and brings the area a frost-free climate all year around. On the eastern side, however, the Jebel Ansariyeh drops off sharply into the Orontes River basin where two of Syria's major cities are located, Aleppo and Damascus.

The eastern side of the Orontes valley abruptly confronts the Anti-Lebanon Mountains which rise to a height

of nine thousand feet and then slant softly like a stage into
the steppes and desert interior, broken only by the Tigris
and Euphrates rivers and their tributaries. The irrigation
which once made this land tillable and which had been
abandoned for centuries because of one conquest after another, is being gradually restored. Today Syria has a surplus of agricultural production, particularly cereals.

Israel is a long narrow strip lying alongside the Mediterranean, with acreage and borders which vary with every
war and peace conference. The coastal plain along the sea
is well-watered and fertile. The south from Beersheba to
the Gulf of Aqaba is an arid section known as the Negev.
The eastern border flanks the Dead Sea, a body of salt
water forty-six miles long and eight miles wide. The surrounding desert at almost thirteen hundred feet below sea
level is the lowest spot on earth. The people of Israel are
predominantly Jews, including some 600,000 so-called
Oriental Jews who had been scattered throughout the
Middle East and North Africa for centuries. Other migrants are from Europe, Russia, and some 40,000 from the
United States. The native-born Israeli, called the "sabra,"
is becoming more and more predominant, naturally.

The people of Iraq include the Marsh Arabs, the pastoral Arabs, the Kurds, and Assyrian Christians. Iraq is,
of course, ancient Mesopotamia, the old, old "Land Between the Rivers." The country is mostly alluvial plains,
flooded every spring, bordered on the northwest by the
towering Zagros Mountains. The countryside lying north
and east of the capital city of Baghdad is the ancient land

of Assyria. The higher hills in the far east are sometimes called Iraqi Kurdistan because of the heavy concentration of Kurds living there.

The picturesque Marsh Arabs, who long ago traded their camels for canoes, live in the extreme south of Iraq in the marsh areas around the mouth of the Tigris-Euphrates. The Marsh Arabs fish—sometimes with nets, sometimes with spears—raise rice, and weave mats for trading purposes. Their chief animal is the water buffalo, which provides milk, meat, and hides. The Marsh Arabs live, in the main, on man-made islands. Their homes usually have arched roofs and are built of reeds cemented together by dung (which also serves as fuel).

The Kurds are a proud, fierce breed of warriors who saw their homeland parcelled out between Iran, Iraq, Syria, and Turkey after World War I and have been fighting intermittently since for the independence they thought they had been promised. Dressed in earth-colored robes and turbans and astride shaggy ponies, the Kurds, when not warring, are farmers and herdsmen in the rough foothills and slopes of the Zagros, something over a million of them in Iraq and most of the remainder in Turkey.

The Arabian Peninsula—ancient Araby of a thousand tales—is about one-fourth the size of the United States and shaped like a giant boot. It is mostly a great sand-covered rock of a plateau which, as it has turned out, is worth its weight in oil wells. The Hejaz Mountains rise on the west coast bordering the Red Sea. In the extreme south, monsoon rainfall permits agriculture. In the north lies an expanse of arid land dotted with spring-watered oases, while in the southeast is the Rub' al-Khali, some four thousand square miles of desolate wilderness, so isolated that no Westerner succeeded in crossing it until the early 1930s. Some of the Rub' al-Khali is pure desert, but there are also broken mountain ridges, rocky plateaus, and areas that resemble the televised pictures of the moon's landscape. The Rub' al-Khali is known as the "Empty Quarter," for that is what it is.

The majority of the Peninsula is taken up with Saudi Arabia, of course, but several smaller national entities cling to space there also: the Yemen Arab Republic and the People's Democratic Republic of Yemen in the southeast; Oman, stretched along the northeast coast of the Arabian Sea; the United Arab Emirates, a coalition of sheikhdoms on the Persian Gulf; Qatar, Bahrain, and Kuwait, also on the Gulf.

The climate of most of the Arabian Peninsula is arid, with extremes of temperature—over 120 degrees F. in the summer and heavy frosts and snow in the mountains. Except for the Yemen Arab Republic and the coastal areas, there is little rainfall. The coastal areas are also notable for extremely high and uncomfortable humidity.

There were, by the last census and rough estimate in some areas, about eight million people living on the Peninsula, almost all of them Arabs, although a few Baluchi and Persians have infiltrated the eastern coastal areas.

The Arabs of the Peninsula differ greatly, due partly to the sections in which they live and partly to their occupations. By far the most numerous of all are the small farmers, the *fellahin*, who live in small villages. Perhaps the heaviest concentration of *fellahin* is in the Yemen Arab Republic, which occupies land that was once the countries of Hadramaut and Saba. The latter is, of course, better known in history as Sheba, made famous by its queen of fabulous beauty, who, the Old Testament says, visited Solomon in his court. This was in the tenth century B.C. Arabs in the cities became Westernized, to some degree, and others have succumbed to the lure of high wages in the oil fields. But Araby is better known in both history and fable for another breed of Arab—the Bedouins, or *Bedu*, in the Arabic language.

These turbanned and bandoleered nomads consider themselves the only true Arabs, the "heirs of glory," and even those who have today strayed into roughnecking on the oil rigs, are fiercely loyal to their tribal leaders and codes. "Fierce" is actually a pretty good adjective to use in describing the *Bedu*, whether he is fighting an enemy, his desert wildness, or the half-tamed camel he rides and with whom he has a hate-love relationship. The camel is a mean, bad-tempered beast who will bite him viciously at any given opportunity, but also is necessary to his very existence.

The Bedouins were the leading edge of the Muslim armies which swept like the hot winds over the Middle East in the wars that converted the land to Islam in the seventh and eighth centuries. During World War I, under the leadership of Lawrence of Arabia, they fought the Turks, who had chosen the Kaiser's side of the conflict, creating a highly successful diversion to keep Ottoman forces out of the European side of the conflict. The accounts of Lawrence's campaigns with his desert forces include one of a dinner he attended with some fifty tribal leaders. The main course was a huge brazier of stew, easily identifiable as mutton by the sheep heads, hair and all, which had been included with most of the rest of the animals.

The fifth area geographically is Egypt and the Sudan. The Sudan stretches from the Egyptian border on the north to the equator on the south, where it has borders with Zaire, Uganda, and Kenya. Its population of some fifteen million is concentrated along the Nile, especially at Khartoum. Much of the rest is desert, rather plentiful with oases and well-traveled by nomads. The climate ranges from hot and arid in the north to very rainy in the equatorial south. The people of the Sudan are a mixture of Arab and African.

The Egyptian is basically Arabic, but differs from those of other neighboring countries, particularly the *fellahin*, who are stockier and lighter of skin than either the Arabs of the Peninsula or the Sudan. Cairo, with four million people, is the nation's largest city, and Alexandria, with a million and a half, the chief port. Almost all of the rest of the country's thirty-seven million people live in villages along the Nile or throughout the Delta, which reaches from Cairo to the sea.

The life of the Egyptian *fellah* has been dictated by the rise and fall of the Nile for millennia. A thousand years or so ago the world's longest river controlled itself and the *fellahin* simply took advantage of its bounty at the will of nature. Today the waters are man-controlled, first by the great Aswan Dam which regulates its flow to the Delta on its course through Egypt by irrigation systems. Throughout much of the Middle East the *fellah* or peasant will live in the same way, in a small village near his small farm, tilling the soil, raising a little stock, seldom in his lifetime venturing more than a few miles from home and content to have it that way. Only the crops and the livestock differ from country to country.

His day begins at dawn with the call from the minaret tower of the mosque—the *muezzin* reminding him that prayer is better than sleep. His family, who most likely all sleep in the same room on cotton mattresses which are rolled up during the day, join him in the morning prayers and have breakfast of milk and tea, cheese and bread.

The children, from age five or six to ten or eleven, will go to an elementary school. Older girl children will help at home with the stock, the chickens, the household chores, or occasionally in the fields when needed. The father and sons head daily for their small plot for the various stages of farming, often raising the water with hand-powered machinery for irrigation, hoeing, and harvesting. Frequently now, with controlled water, they can grow two and sometimes three crops a year.

The Sahara, last of the six regions, lies mainly in Libya, Egypt, and the Sudan, but also includes Morocco, Algeria, and Tunisia. Its three and a half million miles are large enough to blanket the United States and have some left over. Despite movies and some descriptions, the Sahara is not all wind-blown dunes, sand storms, and shifting desert scenery. It has high mountains, deep valleys, and many spring-fed oases. One of them—though a little over-blown to be called an oasis—is known as the Rebiana Sand Sea, in south central Libya. Here deep wells have tapped a reservoir of water believed great enough to irrigate a quarter million acres for two hundred years, which is not long as history goes in the Middle East, but which for the time turns the desert into grain fields and vegetable gardens.

The population of the region designated as the Sahara is roughly thirty-five million people, virtually all of them Arabs except a few Berbers, the original settlers, in Morocco. They comprise about 35 percent of the fifteen million people there and live mainly in the mountain villages. Morocco is, of course, separated from Spain and Europe by only the few miles of the Straits of Gilbraltar and is highly urbanized and Westernized as are its neighbors, Algeria and Tunisia.

The Sahara Desert itself is peopled by villagers in the oases and by nomads who live much as those of other desert areas in the Middle East. The Sahara is the largest desert in the world and has the dubious distinction of, for whatever reason, growing larger every year; it extends itself southward about 150 feet annually.

CHAPTER **X**

The Persian Gulf States

BAHRAIN

KUWAIT

IRAN

IRAQ

QATAR

SAUDI ARABIA

THE UNITED ARAB EMIRATES

BAHRAIN

THE nation of Bahrain is a tiny group of islands in the Persian Gulf with a total land area of 231 square miles, a population estimated at 225,000 people, and a historical lineage going back to 2000 B.C., when it was the site of the ancient civilization of Dilman.

In addition to Bahrain, the dominant island and site of the capital, the other noticeable bits of land in the group are Jazirat Al Muharraq, Umm Na'san, Sitrah, and Nabih Salih. Bahrain is connected to Muharraq by a causeway and with Sitrah by a shallow strait which is dry at low tide. Bahrain is thirty miles long, Muharraq is four. The island group lies only a few miles northwest of the larger island nation of Qatar.

Oil in commercial quantities was found in Bahrain in 1932 via concessions given Socal and Texaco, but production has dwindled to something like 65,000 barrels a day (with a twenty-year reserve) and while this is not trivial and remains the major source of Bahrain's income, the tiny sheikhdom has been intelligently and industriously seeking supplements.

Perhaps the largest refinery in the Middle East is located at Sitrah. It has a capacity of 200,000 barrels a day and is supplied from its Saudi Arabian source by a major pipeline. The Gulf terminal at Sitrah can accommodate today's most modern tankers. Also in cooperation with the Saudis, Bahrain is exploring a new offshore field between the two countries.

And, more recently, Bahrain has made a bid to take over from war-ravaged Beirut as the banking center of the Middle East. According to financial news reports, some thirty international banks, including such giants as Bank of America, Lloyds, First National City, American Express, and Chase Manhattan, have been granted licenses to operate in Bahrain.

The target is, of course, the surplus billions of the oil countries—billions which rise into the hundreds of billions. Bahrain has a number of inducements to offer the big banks (at $25,000 each per license): a stable government, no corporate taxes, no personal taxes, a very liberal society with (contrary to many other Muslim nations) no restrictions on alcohol. The climate isn't very felicitous, with temperatures reaching 105 degrees many days a year, high humidity, and an annual rainfall of under four inches. However, modern business and its personal household live in air-conditioned offices, homes, and automobiles. And the beaches of the Mediterranean are only an hour or two away by plane.

Bahrain's political history had been notably checkered for centuries until the late nineteenth when Britain became interested in the area. Those were the days when England, with her mighty Navy, could and did, as historian Mahan described, send out a ship of the line just to put in an appearance—and to deliver gently "the tap of the lion's paw" to lesser powers, who quickly saw the light. Along with several other Persian Gulf countries at that time, Bahrain's Sheikh al-Khalifah placed Bahrain under English protection in return for giving up any concessions to any other nations.

This arrangement ended on August 14, 1971, when the old treaty was terminated. Bahrain became fully independent to go it on her own, but did sign a treaty of friendship with England the next day. And in September, Bahrain became a member of both the Arab League and the United Nations.

The present ruler of Bahrain is Sheikh Salman bin Hamid al-Khalifah (the Khalifah family has ruled since 1782), who assumed that position in 1961 at the age of twenty-eight. Bahrain has no political parties but the will of the people is made known effectively through a system of political clubs and the ruling sheikh is guided and advised by a Council of Ministers. The ruling family, though, obviously has its prerogatives. Sheikh al-Khalifah has designated his son, Hamad, as heir apparent and Minister of Defense. And the three other important posts on the Council—Prime Minister, Minister of Foreign Affairs, and Minister of Public Security—have gone to a brother, an uncle, and a cousin of the sheikh.

KUWAIT

Kuwait lies at the head of the Persian Gulf, notched in between Iraq and Saudi Arabia like a bite out of a piece of toast. At first glance at least, it should be one of the more pleasant places of the world in which to be born and grow up.

Kuwait's annual income of more than $10 billion means a per capita income for its less than one million native citizens of about $11,000 each a year. This is the highest in the world, or at least the Union Bank of Switzerland so decided after a prolonged study.

Medical attention is free to all in Kuwait, including trips to far-distant specialists. So is education, and this covers food and clothing for the students, including those hundreds who go abroad each year for higher learning. Their needs are ministered from an office in London set up for that purpose.

Kuwait has no income tax, no sales tax, no corporation tax; local telephone calls are free, cigarettes cost under twenty cents a pack, and gasoline the same per gallon. Foreigners are not permitted to own more than 49 percent of any enterprise or any land at all. The present ruler, Sheikh Sabah al-Salim al-Sabah, is probably the highest paid of Kuwait's citizens at about $24 million annually, though this may not necessarily represent the highest individual income in the country.

Housing in Kuwait is virtually free, that is, the government will build its citizen a house, loan him the money to build or buy it himself virtually interest free, or rent it to him at two or three dollars a month. And while that per capita figure of $11,000 does not get clear to the bottom of the class levels there, each Kuwaiti family does have a guaranteed income of $3,000.

All of this, of course, is the result of the discovery of oil in Kuwait in the 1930s. At the beginning of the century Kuwait had a per capita income of about twenty dollars per family and that had not risen a great deal thirty years later. Unlike most of the Middle East, Kuwait is not ancient. In fact, it has no history back of 1800, when it was first settled. Kuwait lies within reach of the historic Tigris-Euphrates valley of Mesopotamia but never was a part of it, turning instead, both by climate and instinct, to the desert of Saudi Arabia, its nomads, and its habits.

History begins for Kuwait around that year of 1800 when several Arabian families of the Anaiza clan migrated from the interior of the Peninsula to the coast, settling what is now Kuwait the city (the name means "little fort") as well as Kuwait the country.

Most of the upper-class families of Kuwait today are descendants of these first few immigrants with the founding names of al-Sabah, as-Zayed, al-Jalahima, and al-Khalifah. The present dynasty—Sabah—dates back to the mid-nineteenth century. The early settlers at that time decided they needed a representative for both local and international affairs, mostly because by that time Kuwait the city had grown to some ten thousand people who made their living from the sea.

In 1899, when the Ottoman Empire began looking with acquisitory eyes at the tiny but prospering entity, then Sheikh Mubarak negotiated a pact with the British, agreeing that Kuwait, in return for protection, would, in effect, have no dealings with other countries without asking the British first. Also under Mubarak the sheikhdom of Kuwait elevated itself to statehood, although it did not become fully independent until 1961.

Early Kuwait was entirely dependent on the sea, for the land, the city, and the countryside was desert, totally without usable water, the rainfall limited to traces in the spring which brought out for a brief moment the thousands of wildflowers before the desert returned to brown sand. There was no grass, no plantlife, no trees except in a few, scattered oases throughout the tiny land only slightly larger than the state of Connecticut.

The sea provided fish, which made up a large share of the daily diet, and a source of income for the merchant princes and their eight hundred-odd *dhows*, who employed most of the nation in shipbuilding, pearling, and trading as far distant as the Red Sea. Before 1940 and the impact of oil money, time had brought little change in Kuwait. The city was walled, with gates which were closed and locked at night. The streets were narrow and dark; Kuwait had no electricity. The town was a popular trading center, with visiting Bedouins, other desert tribesmen, and touring mariners crowding a large central market where everything from dried fish to camels, lace to jewelry was bought and sold. Kuwait rarely saw a Westerner; most were unaware that the West existed. The wealthier Kuwait merchants, however, were relatively sophisticated, frequently with trading representatives in England or on the Continent.

British Petroleum (then the Anglo-Persian Oil Company) had been interested in Kuwaiti oil exploration since before World War I, but didn't act until the early 1930s when Gulf Oil also came looking for concessions. Then in 1933 the two, BP and Gulf, formed an operating company, each holding 50 percent, which negotiated a seventy-five-year lease (later extended seventeen years). Oil was discovered in 1938 but any development was delayed until after World War II. Over the years since, Kuwait's production and the estimate of her reserves have climbed into third place in the Middle East, behind only Saudi Arabia and Iran. And, of course, she now owns the oil fields.

Kuwait is a constitutional monarchy and has been since November of 1962. The Emir is chosen from among members of the Mubarak line of the al-Sabah family, ruling dynasty of the country. He appoints the Prime Minister and the PM names the cabinet, subject to the Emir's approval. Kuwait city is, of course, the capital of the nation and also the residence of more than half the inhabitants. These are primarily Arabs (only about half actually born there), with a sizeable Iranian colony. Kuwait, with its two hundred-odd schools and emphasis on education, has the highest literacy rate in the Middle East—60 percent. Kuwait is hot pretty much the year around, with the temperature reaching 130 degrees in the shade in summer, and only about four inches of rain a year. Most of the country's food is imported; all of the water used to be, but now much of it is supplied through desalination plants, another conferment of oil's bounty.

IRAN

Iran has never been humdrum or insignificant. During its long history there have been very few dull centuries. It is, though, a curious country: extravagantly rich in its history, whimsical in its topography, and careless in its location. In the latter it chose to have borders with Russia, Afghanistan, Pakistan, Iraq, and Turkey, all of which it has quarrelled with spasmodically for centuries. Its land is mostly desert and mountains; almost half of the country is over six thousand feet high, climbing at points up to eighteen thousand feet, and the climate is incredible.

And its native sons have added chapters, or at least pages, to history which are familiar to every schoolgirl and boy today. Cyrus the Great actually founded the country of Persia, and thus created the Persians, by consolidating a lot of dissident small states in southwestern Iran around about 550 B.C. He also added quite a bit of territory, including Babylonia and Sardis. The latter was ruled by the legendary Croesus.

Darius, also called the Great, established himself in history (490 B.C.) by losing the battle of Marathon to the Athenians, who dispatched a runner to Athens with the

news, thus laying the foundation for the marathon run of today's Olympic Games. The distance, incidentally is 26 miles, 385 yards.

And, of course, there was Xerxes, son of Darius, who invaded Greece in the summer of 480 B.C. The Spartans tried to cut him off at the pass of Thermopylae, dying to the man in the attempt. Xerxes went on to Athens where he burned the Acropolis. The Greeks revenged that by routing his fleet in another remembered battle—Salamis.

Today Iran is most notable for its oil. It is one of the Middle East's largest producers, with revenues varying annually around $25 billion, and is possibly the most progressive of the Persian Gulf countries. In 1946, after World War II, the last Soviet occupying troops reluctantly withdrew from Iran, and Britain, too, relaxed a colonial grip, paving the way for independence. After some internal bickering, Iran established a stable government which, since 1963, has conducted a remarkable program of modernization, land distribution to the peasants (feudal estates and Crown properties), promoted a number of reforms, including child care and the emancipation of women. Shahanshah (King of Kings) Muhammad Reza Pahlavi in 1971 created a national Health Corps which provided that students could carry out their required national service by serving as teachers in rural schools, and otherwise campaigned against illiteracy.

The government of the Imperial Government of Iran is a constitutional monarchy with a bicameral parliament and a prime minister, but the monarch is the main decision-maker. The Shah maintains good relations with both the East and the West, visiting both and trading with both. Iran's political ties, though, are with the West.

Iran is one of three countries in the Middle East which is not Arab, nor is it Semitic. It is, however, Muslim, with some 90 percent belonging to the Shi'a sect of Islam instead of the more traditional and orthodox Sunni sect. There are approximately 32 million people in Iran, almost half of whom live in the cities. Also, about half are under fifteen years of age. Some two-thirds of Iran's people are ethnic Iranians who speak either Persian or another of a great assortment of Indo-European languages—Kurdish, Gilanis, Mazandharanis, Lurs, or Baluchis. Most of the remainder speak Turkish, including the former residents of Azerbaijan. There also are smaller ethnic groups of Arabs, Armenians, Jews, and Assyrians.

About 70 percent of Iran is uninhabitable. The country consists generally of a central plateau ranging in height from three to five thousand feet. This plateau is ringed on all sides by mountains, mostly the Zagros and the Elburz. The highest peak in the country, Mount Damavand in the Elburz range, is 18,700 feet high and volcanic. The northern side of the range drops down to the marshy jungle surrounding the Caspian Sea, which is below sea level by about one hundred feet and rapidly shrinking in dimensions.

Much of Iran's interior plateau is a salt swamp—geophysically a phenomenon—bounded by areas of fertile land around the perimeter, and it is in these areas that much of the nation's agriculture is carried on. The immense swamp itself, the Kavir, is so barren, treacherous, and formidable that much of it is not even explored.

Iran also goes to extremes in its climate. The summers are as hot as any place in the world, rising to 130 degrees F. in the interior—and then dropping to minus 20 degrees F. in winter in places, with zero weather quite ordinary. Adding to the pleasures of these extremes is the so-called "Wind of 120 Days" which blows regularly and steadily during the summer, reaching velocities of one hundred miles an hour, carrying tons of sand along and often scouring stone buildings to skeletons.

The country is arid except for the densely populated area along the Caspian Sea coast which is hot and humid, with as much as eighty inches of rainfall annually.

With a total area of 636,000 square miles, Iran is a little larger than Alaska. The capital city is Tehran with a population of almost three million. It is located in the north central part of the country. Other cities are Tabriz, far up near the northwest corner and the borders of Russia and Turkey, half a million people; Shiraz, in the south central part, 340,000; Meshed, in the northeast with a little over half a million; and Abadan, in the southwest, near the borders of Iraq and Kuwait, about 300,000.

Like the country of which it is the capital, Tehran is a city of contrasts, the modern and the old. The downtown streets are thronged with men in business suits and young women government and commercial employees in high heels and short skirts. Near the mosques and in the markets the woman may wear a long black *chador* or veil and the men will be covered in the *gallabia*, the long and usually gray cotton gown which pulls over the head and encompasses from shoulders to ankles. There is evidence everywhere, even in the tiny gardens of the poorer homes, of the traditional Persian love for running water, singing birds, and blooming flowers. Many of the larger residences are magnificently verdant.

Tehran is modern in many ways. It has more than sixty daily international air flights, local flights to the other Iranian cities, and good intercity train and bus service. Phone service is good, the city is reasonably clean and tidy, there are plenty of taxis and, believe it or not, the drivers do not expect to be tipped.

IRAQ

For thousands of years Iraq, originally Mesopotamia, has been the setting for one civilization after another: the Ubadians, Sumerians, Amorites, Assyrians, Persians, the Greeks, the Romans, Islam, the Ottoman, and, lastly, the British Empire.

Iraq finally became independent in 1932 after infinite troubles with the British and the Turks, but that was no guarantee of a serene path as a free nation. Consider the following tortured course:

Faisal Ibn Husain, first chosen king in 1924, ruled through the end of the British mandate and until death in 1933.

His son, Ghazi Ibn Faisal, succeeded and ruled until he was killed in an automobile accident in 1939.

Ghazi's son, Faisal II, ruled both under a regent and in his own right until his assassination in 1958 via a military coup. The Faisal II reign saw the formation of the historic Baghdad Pact, a mutual defense agreement by Iraq, Turkey, Iran, and Pakistan, all of which border Russia, and Great Britain, which does not.

The coup in which both Faisal II and his Prime Minister were killed was led by General 'Abd al-Karim Kassem who proclaimed a republic which never quite materialized. He himself became a de facto dictator, withdrew Iraq from the Baghdad Pact, broke treaties with the United States, and began a mild flirtation with Soviet Russia.

Kassem led the government until February, 1963, when he too was assassinated, in a revolt led by the Ba'ath Party which established a government with General Ahmad Hassan al-Bakr serving as Prime Minister.

Nine months later the new Ba'ath government was forceably kicked out in a coup led by 'Abd al-Salam Muhammad Aref. Aref was killed in a plane crash in April, 1966, and succeeded by his brother, General Abdal Rahman Muhammad Aref.

This regime lasted until July 17, 1968, when the Ba'ath Party, aided by the military, moved back in, ousted General Aref and established government by a Revolutionary Command Council. Hassan al-Bakr returned to become President and chairman of the Council (RCC), which has a relatively small component of civilians and military enacting legislation by decree.

Iraq, with an area of 172,000 square miles, is about the size of California. Its population is something over ten million people, some two million of them Kurds, with lesser minorities of Assyrians, Turkomans, Iranians, Lurs, and Armenians. (The Kurds in the far north, who differ in dress and language, fought for and obtained a partial autonomy.) About 95 percent of the people are of the Muslim faith, with small communities of Christians, Jews, and other sects. Arabic is the most common language used.

Iraq has been described as "a desert floating on a sea of

oil," a description which could equally be applied to other Middle Eastern nations, too. Iraq's entry into the realm of the black gold came in 1925 and a few succeeding years when she granted exploration rights to the Iraq, Mosul, and Basra petroleum companies (all were associated). By 1934 the Iraq company was exporting some oil by pipeline, but the real discoveries did not come until after World War II, and then they came in a flood. By 1970, Iraq was the eighth largest oil producer in the world, and in 1973 she joined the other Middle East nations in a concerted action against the oil companies. Today almost all of the oil operations in Iraq have been nationalized.

Iraq's chief port is Basra, founded in A.D. 36, on the Shatt-al-Arab River, some seventy-five miles from the gulf but open to ocean-going vessels. In northern Iraq the largest city is Mosul, resting on the right bank of the Tigris and opposite the one-time site of proud Nineveh, capital of Assyria.

The capital of Iraq is Baghdad and, with total disdain for the unhappy military-political litany of the government, it remains constant as one of the most beautiful, historic, and romantic cities in the world. It is the seat of government, the financial center of the country, the focal point of industry, center of communications—press, radio, and television—home of a million people, and heir to all the legends of Babylon, Ur, and Nineveh. In a sense, Baghdad is the heart and soul of Iraq.

This 1200-year-old city of Aladdin and Sinbad is divided by the Tigris River into two halves, the western section of Karkh, and Rasafa to the east. Like other large Middle

Eastern cities, Baghdad is a mixture of the new and the very old, in customs, dress, and architecture. There are modern buildings, traffic jams, air pollution, raucous auto horns, blaring radios—all of the amenities of modern civilization—and Saville Row suits and Paris dresses, supper clubs, tennis clubs, swimming clubs, bikinis, and golden tans.

There are also mosques and minarets and the *muezzin* calling the faithful to prayer five times a day, the *gallabia* of the *fellahin* and the flowing robes and turban of the Bedouin. A couple of blocks from the glass and steel skyscraper is the *medina*, the old city, and the *souk*—bazaar or market. In Baghdad the *souk* is miles of little shops winding along the river: shops for buying silver, copper, herbs, perfumes, rugs, robes, jewels and jewelry, furniture, and if you enquire about the purchase of a camel or a horse, you will find a man within earshot who will, quite quickly, guide you to a seller.

QATAR

Even the comparatively modest wealth that the discovery of oil brought to Qatar caught the royal government unprepared. Within a few years the tiny nation's national income climbed from virtually nothing to a billion and a half dollars a year, and various chiefs of government had trouble dealing with the money.

The State of Qatar (its official name) on the Persian Gulf is about 100 miles long and 35 miles wide, somewhat smaller than the state of Massachusetts, all stony, sandy, and barren. The very little bit of underground water is too high in mineral content for irrigation, let alone drinking. Archaeological explorations have established that Qatar was inhabited by people of some sort as early as 4,000 B.C. What they did for water is unknown. Today's residents desalinate it from the ocean.

Oil was discovered in Qatar (best pronounced "gutter," deep in the throat) in 1940 but exports did not begin until 1947 after the confusion from World War II cleared away. Until that time the Qataris made their living by pearl diving, fishing, and nomadic herding. And for almost a century had lived under the benign protection of Britain and the Royal Navy.

Full independence came on September 3, 1971, but the

trouble in handling the new-found wealth began earlier. The sheikhdom has traditionally been ruled by the al-Thani family and there were several changes between the advent of oil and 1960 when Sheikh al-Ahmad assumed the throne. His solution for disposing of the national income was to keep a large share of it for himself and his family, about one-fourth, and by the 1970s this had reached a sizeable sum. Some of this he spent on his yacht, which had formerly been a commercial cruise liner, and on renting large jet passenger planes for his private use. He also arranged that every male member of the al-Thani family receive an annual income of $7,000 a year from birth. This is not really as presumptuous as it sounds; there were some five hundred-odd male al-Thanis and by including wives and daughters you arrive at a large percentage of the native-born Qatari population.

Like other Gulf-side rulers whose country tails off into the lands of Araby, Sheikh al-Ahmad had the desert in his blood and in 1972 when he was away on an extended trip there, camel racing and falcon hunting, he was deposed by his deputy and prime minister (and kinsman) Sheikh Khalifa bin Hamad al-Thani. The reason for the coup, though never stated, was that al-Ahmad's son had been planning his own revolt against both his father and Khalifa, to the extent of importing large quantities of arms for the purpose. The coup was family-arranged and both al-Ahmad and son were exiled to Dubai, of the Emirates, and the hospitality of the ruler there, who happened to be al-Ahmad's father-in-law.

Sheikh Khalifa proved an unusual ruler immediately.

He reduced the salary of the immediate crown family to a quarter million a year, raised the pay of all government workers 20 percent, and changed the $7,000 annual allowance to all male al-Thanis to start at twelve years instead of at birth. The government of Qatar had sold many homes to its citizens on long-term mortgages. Sheikh Khalifa wrote off the balance of payments on all of them. He also built schools and hospitals.

The State of Qatar occupies all of a small peninsula jutting into the Persian Gulf and its 6,000 square miles are mostly flat desert broken by a few limestone ridges. The amount of rainfall is hardly worth measuring and the climate is hot—120 degrees—most of the year and humid along with it. Only about half the total population of 140,000 are natives, the rest immigrants attracted to the oil fields, including a fair number of Palestine refugees.

Doha, the capital and major city of Qatar, has been transformed by oil money from a muddy little village into a small modern city with paved streets, electricity, and modern buildings; it even has a Chamber of Commerce. It is on the east coast, about center, and has a shallow port. The major port where oil shipments are handled is Umm Said, twenty miles southward. Qatar is a member of the Arab League, the United Nations, and OPEC. It has friendly relations with its neighbors, and has no real outside political alignments, though it still looks upon Britain as a best friend.

SAUDI ARABIA

SAUDI Arabia is the quintessence of the Middle East, the birthplace of Muhammad and Islam, the land of Araby and the land of Mecca, the Holy City. Five times each day the Muslim faithful, no matter where they may be, face toward Mecca and the Great Mosque there, and supplicate themselves in prayer.

In years past the mention of Saudi Arabia would bring up, in instant reflex, the image of the Bedouin in flowing robes, astride his camel, head bowed to the sandstorm. Today, if the Bedouin and his desert steed are in the picture at all, they will be stage props to the main subject—the steel struts of the oil rig. Saudi Arabia, according to most calculators, is the world's third leading oil producer and exporter of oil, with government revenues in the neighborhood of $30 billion a year. Production comes from fourteen Persian Gulf fields, the three most important of which are Ghawar, Abqaiq, and Sanfaniya. Ghawar is the world's largest oil field and Sanfaniya the world's largest offshore operation.

Oil was discovered in commercial quantities in 1938 by an exploration company which had been put together by Standard Oil of California (Socal), and called the Arabian American Oil Company—Aramco. After ten years

Socal divvied up Aramco with three other of the Seven Sisters of the oil world and they deftly managed to freeze everyone else out of the Saudi Arabian oil picture. The four were Socal, Exxon, Texaco, and Mobil. The first three owned 30 percent each. Mobil wanted and took only 10 percent, a move she deeply regretted in later years because Aramco became profitable beyond all belief.

The result of the Aramco discoveries was, of course, a great influx of American oil men to Arabia and the oil fields—management officials, engineers, technicians, and roustabouts, usually accompanied by their families. In his book *The Seven Sisters*, British journalist Anthony Sampson describes the phenomenon thus:

> . . . there rose up in the desert, on the edge of the oil fields, the most amazing of all company towns: the compound at Dhahran which provided the headquarters of the Arabian American Oil Company or Aramco. Bungalow houses sprang up in neat rows, with creepers up the walls and green lawns alongside the desert, and a complete suburb formed itself with a baseball park, a cinema, swimming pools and tennis courts. It was an astonishing optical illusion, looking like a small town from Texas or California, whence many of the inhabitants came; except that it was ringed round with a high barbed-wire fence, with beyond it an expanse of limitless desert, with only a few oils wells and pipelines to break the monotony.
>
> In this isolated outpost the employees or "Aramcons" as they called themselves, soon acquired a special kind of character or nationality of their own, caught between the loyalties to two countries and to four companies. As one of their early employees described it: "Aramco was, in effect, the neurotic child of four parents, subject to the

whims, qualms and jealousies of each." The sense of un-
certainty in this desert community was increased by the
anger of the Arabs at American policy toward Israel and
the eccentric demands of the Saudi Kings.

The four owners of Aramco and the Saudi Arabian government recently completed an arrangement whereby
Saudi Arabia purchased the last 40 percent of Aramco.
Under this "negotiated takeover," the Aramcon force of
some 1,600 persons, largely Americans, was gradually aug-
mented by two hundred or so persons, including Saudis.
American management continues to operate the oil business, to enlarge exploration activities, and also to establish
an electrification network in the eastern section of Saudi
Arabia, including the capital of Riyadh and the Arabian
(or Persian) Gulf Coast. The four oil companies comprising Aramco continue, of course, to buy their usual
amounts of oil.

There is a brief footnote to the oil history of Saudi
Arabia: the big desert country has two tiny "neutral
zones" set aside in arguments over national boundaries.
One Saudi Arabia shares with Kuwait and it is there that
the late J. Paul Getty, often catalogued as the richest man
in the world, grabbed up enough leases to make his first
billion.

There is some evidence that Saudi Arabia was once a
fertile land, but as far back as today's knowledge of history
goes, it has always been a desert with small pockets of
oasis civilization. These existed for, and often in spite of,
a thousand nomadic tribes who lived by the camel, trading the beast and its by-products, feeding on its milk and

flesh, and wearing its hair and skin. Of course they also lived by raiding the weak and unwary—other tribes or even the oasis itself.

The earliest recorded government of Saudi Arabia was the Minaean Kingdom which flourished around 1200 B.C. The dynasty which presently rules the country is the House of Sa'ud, which goes back to the fifteenth century when the ancestors of the present King and Prime Minister left their homes on the Persian Gulf and settled not too far from what is now Riyadh, the capital. Actual conquest by the Sa'ud family began in 1744 with Muhammad Ibn Sa'ud and was not fully accomplished until the early part of the present century under the rule of Abdul Aziz Ibn Abdul Rahman al-Faisal al-Sa'ud, better known by the patronym of Ibn Sa'ud. He died peacefully in 1953 and his ultimate successor was King Faisal. He was assassinated on March 25, 1975, by one of his nephews and was succeeded by King Khalid Ibn Abd al-Aziz al-Sa'ud.

Measured from the Wadi al-Siran on the Saudi Arabian-Jordan border, the Arabian Peninsula, of which Saudi Arabia constitutes four-fifths, stretches more than a thousand miles south and east, making the country about a third as large as the United States. (A *wadi* is the valley of a stream which is dry except in the rainy season when it may flash-flood in a matter of minutes.)

Saudi Arabia has its own mixed bag of geography, vegetation, and climate. The narrow coastal strip along the Red Sea, known as the Tihama (or lowland) is largely barren. From this coastal area the land rises abruptly into the Hejaz Mountains, in whose passes are located both Mecca and Medina, holy cities of Islam, then slopes gently eastward into the Najd, or center of Araby, a country of shallow valleys and abrupt ridges, usually covered with sand. Nefud, the area to the north, gets some rainfall, and has a few wells in scattered, cultivated oases. South of the Najd lies the Rub' al-Khali or Empty Quarter—thousands of miles of desert which will not support life of any kind.

Most of the east coast of Saudi Arabia, which lies along the Persian Gulf (called the Arabian Gulf in Saudi Arabia) is flat. It is known as the al-Hasa and is the scene of the major oil fields and the oil town of Dhahran. After quitting the Hejaz Mountains, Saudi Arabia is almost entirely desert. There are no permanent rivers. Rainfall is erratic and will total between two and four inches annually, except in Asir, near the South Yemen border which gets up to twelve inches. During the summer the heat is intense, frequently climbing to over 120 degrees, with high humidity on both coasts. And then in winter the temperature will drop below freezing in the central and northern areas.

The Saudi Arabians are ethnically Arabs, but over the centuries there has been an admixture of Turks, Iranians, Indians, and Africans, many of whom came to Mecca as pilgrims and remained to become Arabs.

Population of the country is six or so million. Half of the people live in the cities and of the rest, one quarter are farmers and one quarter nomadic Bedouins. The million and a half-odd farmers toil on the entire tillable land area in Saudi Arabia—.02 percent of the nation's total acreage.

The city of Jidda on the Red Sea is Saudi Arabia's diplomatic capital, port for Mecca, and largest city, with around half a million people. Riyadh, inland, is the royal capital and almost as large, followed by Mecca and Medina with 250,000 and 150,000 each, respectively.

Saudi Arabia is considered to be America's best friend in the Arab world. The United States sells the Saudis arms and aircraft, trains their young men in the use of the equipment, and the two countries cooperate otherwise in the fields of education, agriculture, science and technology, and industrialization. More than 3,000 young Saudis have studied in U.S. schools and colleges.

THE UNITED ARAB EMIRATES

In the late 1700s the pirates became so noxious around the sharp spit of land which projects its pointed snout from Araby into the Persian Gulf that the patience of the British grew thin and they sent the Royal Navy on a corrective mission.

The initial expedition was successful but the mopping up was not concluded until 1835 when all seven sheikhs of the area agreed to abstain from pouncing on each other and anyone else who ventured close enough. And in 1853 all of the sheikhdoms jointly signed virtually the same treaty of protection and friendship that Britain was collecting from most of the other small principalities of the Arabian side of the Gulf. England was interested in the area because it could be used as a gateway to her colonial domain of India.

This four hundred-mile projection, which actually separates the Persian Gulf from the Gulf of Oman, has been, over the years, known variously as the Trucial Sheikhdoms, Trucial States, Trucial Coast, and Trucial Oman.

Today, it is known—and has been since 1971—as the United Arab Emirates, an independent nation composed of the same seven sheikhdoms, now almost entirely peaceable. It is the eighteenth member of the United Arab

League and the 132nd member of the United Nations. The UAE covers an area of 32,000 square miles (about the size of Maine) and has an estimated population of 240,000.

The seven components are Abu Dhabi, Dubai, Sharjah, Ajman, Umm al-Quwain, Ras al Khaimah, and Fujairah. Abu Dhabi is the largest, the capital, and very oil rich. Dubai and Sharjah also have oil, but in lesser quantities.

The relative importance of the Emirates is reflected in the government: the Sheikh of Abu Dhabi, which is the wealthiest and largest, was named President in the first leadership arrangement of the Emirates, and his chief advisor was named Foreign Minister. The Sheikh of Dubai, the next in size and the commercial center of the Emirates, was named Vice President and his son Prime Minister. All of the rulers make up the Supreme Council. Legislative authority is vested in the National Council and there is a system of courts.

The class system of the Emirates is pretty well defined. At the top, of course, are the royal families, wealthy relatives, and friends. Below them, and probably next in importance, is a sizeable group of what is probably best called advisors. While the British withdrew from any official domination of the seven sheikhdoms in 1971, the influence lingers on and the Arab rulers definitely prefer it that way. These advisors, members of what might be termed the white and khaki-collar class, advise on foreign, financial (including oil), and internal security affairs. They are military commanders and subordinates, industry managers, engineers, health and social service advisors,

almost entirely English; they still do mostly the same
things they have done for a century but now do them on
contract, operating in areas where the local people lack
skills, education, and confidence. Slightly under the advisors are the well-to-do merchants and traders. And then
the bulk of the people, semiskilled and unskilled laborers,
many of them Iranians, Pakistanis, Indians, Baluchs, attracted largely by oil field salaries.

Oil was discovered in Abu Dhabi in 1958-60. Prior to
that time the Trucial States' economy was at a barely sub-
sistence level, based on agriculture, sheep and goat herding, fishing and trading. The combined income of the
seven sheikhdoms was about $1.7 million, derived mostly
from oil exploration rights and British government grants.

Oil exports began in 1962 and, by 1975, Abu Dhabi
emerged with one of the higher per capita incomes in the
world (based on actual citizenship) with an annual oil
income of at least $3.5 billion.

The first ruler, Sheikh Zayed bin Sultan al-Nhayyan is
a member of a dynasty which settled Abu Dhabi in the
late 1770s when a water well was brought in on an island
off the coast. By the 1880s some thirty of the al-Nhayyan
clan had settled on farms around the Buraymi Oases at
al-'Ayn, in the eastern part of Abu Dhabi.

It was not until after oil was discovered that members of the al-Nhayyan family, including the governor,
Sheikh Zayed, moved to Abu Dhabi, the capital. Zayed,
the first President, has never really become urbanized
and frequently disappears into the desert for weeks at
a time, returning to al-'Ayn, the home of his youth, and

his real loves—Arabian horses, racing camels, riding and living the life of a Bedouin (which he is in part), and falcon hunting. His son, Khalifah, was named his heir apparent in the traditional move to maintain the dynasty.

The waters of the Persian Gulf off the coast of the UAE are extremely shallow, with numerous small islands and reefs. The climate is arid and hot, with very high humidity. The capital of both Abu Dhabi and the UAE is the city of Abu Dhabi with 85,000 people. The principal port and center of commerce is Dubai, about the same size, in the Emirate of the same name. It is located at the head of a deep channel and has a new deep-water harbor known as Port Rashid. Sharjah is the third best developed of the Emirates, due largely to a Royal Air Force station there. All of the seven Emirates are securely united by a share-the-wealth program, which has been as effective as it might be thought unusual. Education and medical care is free. The Emirates are connected by a coastal highway which runs also to al-'Ayn. Oil exploration projects either in all of the individual Emirates or just offshore have been started.

CHAPTER XI

The Fertile Crescent and Turkey

ISRAEL

JORDAN

LEBANON

SYRIA

TURKEY

ISRAEL

THE Romans conquered and abolished the largely Jewish state of Palestine during the years of the first and second century after Christ, and the Jews scattered all over the earth, quite literally. During the years after, many of them converted to Christianity, to Islam, and to pagan cults. But always there was a remnant which clung to the old belief, the old customs and rituals, the old orthodoxy.

The Jews were alternately welcomed, tolerated, scorned, and persecuted. They were peddlers and prime ministers, lived in palaces and ghettos. During the years between the Romans and the return to the ancient homeland, two little-known Jewish states were attempted. The first, in Yemen early in the sixth century, was ruled by converted Arabs of the southern part of the Arabian peninsula. The other, two centuries later, was near the mouth of the Volga River, where again the rule had to be given to others, this time to the ferociously warlike Kazakhs, who had been converted from heaven knows what. Neither attempt at establishing permanency lasted long. Simply through staying together, however, by the latter part of the nineteenth century, the Jews of Eastern Europe had what amounted to almost a separate nation,

complete with their own language, Yiddish. It was during
this time that the Viennese journalist Theodor Herzl
wrote *A Jewish State*.

Herzl's book and the stir it created among international
Jewry, plus the always latent, emotional pull, resulted in
the organization and meeting of the first Congress of the
Zionist Movement, which was held in Basle, Switzerland,
in 1897. The aim and intent of the Zionists was from the
first, of course, the return to the Holy Land, the Home
Land, back to the River Jordan, to Jerusalem and Beersheba and the Red Sea.

The word "Zion" (or "Sion") comes from a section of
the city of Jerusalem so-named, but has come to be sym-
bolic of the entire city and even the entire Holy Land.
The word "Zionism" was coined by a Russian, according
to historians, but it was made popular at the first Congress
by Herzl, who defined Zionism as "striving to create for
the Jewish people a home in Palestine secured by public
law."

There have been many thousands of words written in
the great debate over whether the Jews had a legal and
moral right to return to Israel. The debate hasn't ended;
it probably never will.

Several things can be readily established, however. Just
prior to World War I and when the Ottoman Empire, of
which Palestine was a part, became known as the "Sick
Man of Europe," Palestine became the "Forgotten Man
of the Middle East" as well. There was little law to protect
the farmer on his few acres of land from either the raiding
Bedouin, who destroyed his crop and stole his stock, or

THE PALESTINE PROBLEM

TURKEY

SYRIA

CYPRUS

• Aleppo

N
W E
S

Mediterranean Sea

Tripoli

LEBANON
BEIRUT ⊕

Sidon • DAMASCUS ⊕

Golan
Heights

Acre
Haifa
Tiberias • Sea of Galilee
Caesaria •

Tel Aviv •
West
Bank

ISRAEL ⊕ AMMAN
JERUSALEM JORDAN
Hebron •
GAZA STRIP
Dead Sea

SUEZ
CANAL

Negev
Desert

EGYPT

Sinai
Peninsula

Aqaba

SAUDI ARABIA

Gulf of Suez

Gulf of Aqaba

Red Sea

⬚ Disputed Territory,
Occupied by Israel

the rapacious landlord, who cheated him at every turn. The peasants were pretty much forced into the new serfdom of tenant farming and the result was the accumulation of vast holdings by owners who lived in the urban centers. The peasants quite naturally allowed their land to first deteriorate and then they simply abandoned it. In the early part of the twentieth century, for instance, most of the hundreds of acres in the once-rich Jezreel Valley belonged to just two persons, the Turkish Sultan and a rich Syrian banker; little of it was properly farmed.

The movement back to the land in Palestine actually began in 1887 when a group of Jewish families living in Jerusalem bought a large tract of land on the Sharon Plain and established the village of Petah Tikva. Others followed—first a trickle, then a wave. After World War I when Palestine was under British Mandate, the London government first encouraged immigration and then backed away when the Arabs suddenly became nationalistically concerned, but no one could stop the flood which poured in after the Hitler pogroms began. The Jewish population in Palestine jumped from 56,000 in 1923 to 608,000 in 1946 and probably increased another fifty thousand by the time of the partitioning.

Today there are some 3.3 million, 50 percent of them "sabras," that is, native-born to Israel; that means a nation with 50 percent of its populace under thirty years of age.

The Jews claim they came by the land they now live on by accepted legal means. Official figures published by the British Mandatory Administration just before turning over that responsibility to the United Nations, on the ownership of the land reserved for the new nation, were: Jewish by purchase, 8.6 percent; Arab-owned, 3.3 percent; abandoned, 16.9 percent; the remaining 70-plus percent belonged to the government, i.e. originally to the Ottoman Empire, then to the Mandate, then to the Israeli government. Most of the 70 percent, by the way, was made up of the Negev Desert, semiarid and then-uninhabited land.

The vote by the United Nations General Assembly on partitioning Palestine came on November 29, 1947. Britain relinquished her mandate at 6 P.M. Eastern U.S. time on May 14, 1948. At 6:01 P.M. the Jewish authorities in Palestine declared the establishment of the nation. At 6:11 P.M. the United States officially recognized the new government. Russia quickly followed, as did other Western nations.

The partition divided Palestine into six parts. Three of them, comprising 56 percent, went to Israel. Three others, or 43 percent, went to the Arabs. The city of Jerusalem was to be held as an international zone administered by the UN. (The first Arab-Israeli clash came almost immediately, followed by subsequent Arab-Israeli wars. See Chapter III.)

Israel of today is considerably different from the country the Jewish people took over on that spring day of 1948, quite literally. The desert has brought productive farms, many of them the cooperative *kibbutzim*, around bustling settlements. Swampy marshlands are today verdant valleys of orchards, vineyards, and produce gardens. A city which did not exist at the time of independence—Tel Aviv—now has a population of 365,000 people. A port on the Mediterranean, which didn't exist either, was dredged out and constructed, and today this port, Haifa, supports more than 215,000 people. Mount Carmel in the background has been developed into both a residence and resort spot and its slopes provide some unparalleled views of the blue-green Mediterranean.

In 1950, Israel proclaimed Jerusalem as its capital but the United States and most other countries do not recognize this, nor Israel's sovereignty over the city, and maintain their embassies in Tel Aviv, the newly created city.

Israel's borders have changed with each war, but it is still only about the size of New Jersey. The new country stretches 260 miles from north to south; east to west it varies from ten to about sixty-five miles. There are four distinct geographical regions: the coastal plains, the central mountains, the Jordan Valley, and the Negev Desert in the south. The Negev comprises half the nation's area and is to some degree being reclaimed through irrigation. Mount Meron is the highest spot in Israel and the Dead Sea the lowest, 3,963 above and 1,302 below sea level, respectively.

In the Negev the weather gets very hot in summer and it can be cold in winter. The north and central mountains have a pleasant climate. The coastal regions are moderate in winter, hot and humid in summer. The rainfall, which is concentrated in the winter months, varies from 25-30 inches in the north, 19-21 around Tel Aviv, and drops down to a trace in the desert.

Israel is not a land for starry-eyed romanticists, but rather one of practical, down-to-earth realists. It is a land of hard work, of tough military service for both men and women. But it is also a pleasant land. The National Theater and other producing companies perform for capacity audiences—Shakespeare, Shaw, Ibsen, and the modern writers, all of whose works have been translated into Hebrew. There are concerts, from modern rock-and-roll to symphony and chamber music. And museums, of course, and restaurants, and nights clubs. In Tel Aviv's Ramat Gan Stadium crowds of sixty thousand watch football (soccer) matches. Tennis, swimming, and hockey are usual and popular.

There are mountains and lakes and beaches for anyone drawn to the outdoors, a vast desert to explore, and always the strong pull of the magnet of antiquity, a sense of treading where some remote ancestor might have put his foot three thousand years ago.

JORDAN

THE Dead Sea is really a salt lake about forty-five miles long and three to ten miles wide, thirteen hundred feet deep, and also thirteen hundred feet below sea level. Like a thousand other spots in Jordan, the Dead Sea abounds in historical facts and legends, many of them endlessly fascinating.

The River Jordan flows into the Dead Sea after dividing Israel and Jordan. (The boundary runs right down the middle of the sluggish stream.) Near the northern end of this saltiest body of water in the world is Jerusalem, shrine of both Israeli and Muslim, and the legendary Jericho, once destroyed by Joshua.

Also at the north end of the Dead Sea once existed the village of Qumran, near which have been found over the past thirty-odd years the famous Dead Sea Scrolls.

Qumran flourished, to one degree and another, at least as far back as a thousand years before Christ. In the seventh century or so B.C., it was a fortified city. More importantly, in the century before and the century after Christ, it is believed to have been the home of the Essenes, a Jewish religious sect known for their skills as healers and a distaste for the sacrificial practices of the Maccabees, then the leading Jewish sect. The Essenes were vegetarians and they also were obviously educated thinkers and historians, for they either wrote or collected, apparently, most of the Scrolls.

Far more recent legend tells that a young shepherd seeking a straying member of his flock in the year 1947 shied a rock into a cave and was startled by the tinkle of shattered pottery. Venturing in, he found a number of ancient jars and in one of them discovered a manuscript written on leather. Eventually, when the boy's family had the highly unusual wisdom to take the scroll to an expert instead of using it for a table mat, it proved to be by far the earliest known version of the Biblical Book of Isaiah. The find triggered a general hunt through the caves which abound the sand hills around what was once the fortified city of Qumran and an extensive set of digs within the site of the ancient city itself.

Some two hundred caves have been explored on the banks above the waterline of the Dead Sea, and they have returned scores of documents of tremendous historical interest, including the Isaiah script, and other Biblical manuscripts predating any known others by centuries, ancient hymns of thanksgiving, a code of behavior for the Essenes, documents in Greek and Aramaic, one Hebraic papyrus dating back to the seventh or eighth century B.C., and enough parallels in the Qumran writing with the Gospel of St. John to suggest that possibly both he and his cousin Jesus were Essenes for at least a while.

The Hashemite Kingdom of Jordan was previously Transjordan, created under mandate after World War I.

Modern Jordan, then, came into being in 1947 when Israel was created, and was slightly enlarged in 1950.

Jordan is a constitutional monarchy with about 37,500 square miles of total area (a little bigger than the state of Indiana) and an estimated population of two and a half million people. Physically, most of Jordan lies on a plateau some two to three thousand feet above sea level and is about 12 percent arable. The nation is bordered by Syria, Iraq, Saudi Arabia, and, of course, Israel. All of the boundaries are tenuous, but Jordan, after many tense moments in the past, manages good relations with three out of four of its neighbors. And her relations with Israel are better than other adjacent Arab nations.

Jordan has always been one of the unrich nations of the Middle East and the first ruler, Abdullah Ibn al Hussein, tried, when his country was first created, to merge with either Syria or Iraq, but had no takers. The limited western portions of the country are fertile with crops of small grain, vegetables, and many tropical fruits. This agriculture occupies the attentions of about 40 percent of the nation's labor force and returns in the neighborhood of 20 percent of its financial return.

Industry, which accounts for about 12 percent of Jordan's domestic production, is largely clustered around the capital city of Amman, on the west bank of the Jordan. At the present much of the industry is weaving and food manufacture, but industrial income from heavier industry—petroleum refining, cement making, and phospate mining—is increasing, particularly the latter, due to recent discoveries of large deposits.

Jordan is ruled by a monarch, the present one King Hussein, who took the throne in May, 1952, following the assassination of his father and the removal from the throne of his elder brother for medical reasons.

Hussein is England-educated and reared, and, contrary to usual royal customs, in moderate circumstances simply because the ruling family was poor right along with the rest of the country. The legislative assembly consists of two houses, Senate and Representatives. Press and private opinions are free and there is no discrimination by either race, religion, or language. Both Arabic and English are taught in schools. The throne of the kingdom devolves by male descent in the family or dynasty of the first ruler, Abdullah Ibn al Hussein. The present king has been married three times—to Sherifa Deena, to English-born Antoinette Avril Gardner, and to Ali Toukan. His first marriage produced a daughter, the second two sons and a daughter. Hussein has, however, designated his younger brother, Hassan, to be heir to the crown.

Amman, the capital, lies in the north central part of the city and has had its own moments in history. The first settlers, along about 1200 B.C., were drawn there probably by the abundance of water from many springs. After some years the town had achieved such a reputation for wickedness that its doom had been foretold by the prophets of the time, and David (the name means "beloved" in Hebrew), second King of the Hebrews, found it useful to order Uriah the Hittite to lead an attack on the town. It was an order which meant certain death, and given because David wanted to—and did—marry Uriah's beautiful

wife Bathsheba. Much later the city was captured and renamed Philadelphia or Philadelphis, after its conquerer,
one of the Ptolemys. And later, during Roman rule, it
reached sufficient importance to achieve an amphitheater
seating six thousand people, still in use today. Like Rome,
incidentally, the city is built on seven hills.

Today the city of Amman has a quarter of a million and
a few more people, modern buildings, traffic jams, inade-
quate transportation—all the pleasantries of civilization—
but also parks and schools, a great leaning toward sports
and games, radio and television.

Ninety percent of the Jordanian people are Arabs, about
half rural and half urban, and the normal five percent desert nomads who roam at will over the borders of Syria and
Saudi Arabia.

Jordan absorbed thousands of Palestine refugees but has
not the resources to take in more. They camp on her borders and have used her territory to stage raids against
Israel. The government of King Hussein maintains an
uneasy balance between his neighbors and the West he
must depend on for both aid and markets.

LEBANON

To most of the world the tiny nation of Lebanon meant its capital of Beirut, a city of cliches, the "most" of everything in the Middle East: most beautiful, most charming, most cosmopolitan, most sophisticated, most modern, most traffic jams. When the land of Lebanon leaves the lovely beaches of the Mediterranean it very quickly climbs into the high Lebanese Mountains. One might—and the livelier of the well-to-do young frequently did—take to the mountains for snow skiing in the morning and race back down for water skiing in the afternoon.

Beirut was an international city where many of the great corporations, banks, and business syndicates of the world maintained offices to monitor the trade of the Middle East and often the Far East as well. It had glamorous modern hotels, beach clubs, the best restaurants where the best food—Middle Eastern, French, or Oriental—was served in gardens open to the skies and brightened with flowering bougainvillea, or maybe up a narrow stairway to a tiny room known only to the old customers. The city, restaurants, and markets abounded in melons and other fresh fruits, artichokes, fresh vegetables, meats, and sweets. There was a large wealthy set of native Middle Easterners in Beirut, landowners from feudal times, financiers, professional people, and a large foreign colony whose lives were brightened by expense accounts. Lebanon has a literacy rate of almost 90 percent, several advanced schools, including the American University, and most of the upper classes speak three or four languages. The women are liberated—at least for the Middle East.

That, of course, is Beirut in the past tense, the Lebanon that was. With the civil war which erupted in Lebanon in 1975, the glory and beauty of Beirut, and much of the rest of Lebanon's civilization, became a concrete wilderness of mortar-wrecked buildings. Both business and fun ceased in Beirut and Lebanon, and with peace it would take years to rebuild. (See Chapter III.)

Along with its rather flagrant opulence, Beirut had its other classes, too, of course—the laborer who struggled up the hill with a refrigerator strapped to his back, equated with his patient donkey, both heavily laden with the cargo of freighters at the dock. There were ugly slum tenement sections of the city, and beggars. But Beirut never seemed to have the grinding misery so obvious in many other Middle Eastern cities, or at least not until one noticed the Palestine refugee camps ringing the city and strung out along the road to the airport, where thousands lived in tents and packing crate huts—and had lived since the partitioning of Palestine in 1947.

Lebanon (may her troubles cease) lies on the eastern shore of the Mediterranean, virtually surrounded by Syria on the north and east. On the south she shares a border with Israel. Back of Lebanon's narrow coastal plain are the high Lebanese Mountains, followed by the fertile

Beqaa Valley and then the Anti-Lebanon Mountains which extend to the Syrian border.

The area of Lebanon is about 4,000 square miles, making the country slightly smaller than the state of Connecticut. The total population is something over three million, one-third of which lives in Beirut, the capital—or did, before thousands left, some of the foreign colony by guarded evacuation.

Outside of Beirut (and the seaport of Tripoli, with a population of about 130,000) most of the Lebanese are rural and live by agriculture: fruits, wheat, corn, olives, potatoes, onions. Twenty-seven percent of Lebanon's area is tillable. Sixty-four percent is desert and the rest heavily forested.

Lebanon was the historical home of the Phoenicians who, a thousand years or so before Christ, moved there from Crete and built such legendary cities as Tyre, Sidon, and Byblos. The Phoenicians were famous as navigators and traders who foraged as far as Spain and established outposts in Carthage and Utica. They were also skilled architects and artists, though probably their greatest one achievement was the invention of the alphabet. Then the Greeks and the Persians came along, conquered and absorbed them.

Certainly the destruction of its country is nothing new to the Lebanese and, when the battles which have raged through Beirut and the neighboring hills do finally cease, they will find themselves with yet another giant task of restoration—physically, commercially, and politically.

SYRIA

SYRIA has had really more than its share of adventurers down through its thousands of years of history, among them a lady named Zenobia, renowned for both her beauty and ambition. Her husband, Septimius Oldenathus, ruled the city-state of Palmyrus, some sixty miles northeast of Damascus, in the A.D. 260s. Oldenathus ambitiously conquered all of the areas within reach, and when he was murdered and Zenobia took charge, she reached out even farther. When she finally conquered all of Syria and Egypt and declared herself "Queen of the East," it was a little too much for the Romans, who looked on that territory as their own backyard, not to mention breadbasket.

So the Roman, Lucius Domitius Aurelianus, otherwise Emperor Aurelian, gave her five years of local glory and then went in with the legions.

Aurelian defeated the Queen's forces at the Orantes River and, according to legend, Zenobia escaped to Palmyra. There she disguised herself as a desert tribesman and rode out of the city on a racing camel. She could not, apparently, conceal her proud, queenly bearing and was followed and captured while attempting to cross the Euphrates River.

Faced with this same situation, Cleopatra had turned
to the poisonous asp, but Zenobia preferred to live. She
was taken to Rome by Aurelian and, clad in silken robes
and golden chains, she was paraded through the streets,
still proud, still beautiful. She lived out her life in Rome
on a generous allowance from the government.

Today Syria has no Zenobias, and Palmyra is a dead city
of spectacular ruins, beautiful in the memories of past
splendor. Syria is a land of some seven milion people,
about the size of South Dakota, and with all the normal
Middle European contrasts, that is, fertile plains mixed in
with mountains and deserts. It is primarily agricultural
and stock raising—small grains, fruits, vegetables, lamb,
mutton, beef, textiles, and wool. There is some industry:
milling and oil refining, textile and glassware manufac-
turing, cement making, tobacco curing, and sugar refining.
Syria has only minuscule oil production but collects royalties from much of Saudi Arabia's vast production which
travels by pipeline across Syria to the sea.

Modern Syria is two-thirds desert. The northern desert
sections in Roman times were irrigated by canals leading
from the Euphrates, but these were long ago destroyed by
invaders—of which there were many—and are just now
being restored. In the spring, briefly, the fields bloom
gaily with myriad flowers. Today's agricultural area lies
in a thirty-mile-wide strip which stretches three hundred miles from almost the Jordan border to almost the
Turkish.

It is in this area also that lie Syria's four major population centers: Damascus, Aleppo, Hama, and Homs. Only

Latakia, a modern port, is on the eighty-mile Mediterranean coastline.

Aleppo is the commercial capital of Syria and, with more than 400,000 people, rivals Damascus, the political capital, in size. The city has been a caravan center for hundreds of years and enjoys the dubious distinction of having been sacked by Tamerlane around A.D. 1400, one of many cities he laid waste.

While Aleppo has many modern amenities—good hotels and modern stores—to go with its commercial aspect, it is chiefly famous for its seemingly endless miles and miles of *souks*—small, twisting streets crammed with little shops which sell almost anything imaginable. The *souks* in Aleppo date back to the thirteenth century, and the streets and shops there are covered with vaulted stone roofs, pierced at intersections for light. Much too narrow for autos, the streets are always—or seem to be—crowded with customers of a dozen races and costumes, pull carts, and bicycles.

Damascus, the capital, is one of the richest cities in the world in its ancient history. Here Paul, once Saul, was briefly blinded by a flash of light and converted to Christianity. It was to the present site of Damascus, or near it, that Adam and Eve repaired after being evicted from the Garden of Eden, and near here that Cain slew Abel. Noah lived in Damascus, as did Abraham; in later times it was visited by Jesus Christ.

Today it is a thriving, modern city of half a million, banded by a circle of verdant gardens which have been irrigated by the River Barada as it flows through the city.

It is a place of modern hotels, embassies, night clubs, and tourists. It also has its *souks*, though not as many or picturesque as those of Aleppo, and a great mosque, the Omayyad, whose towers and dome dominate the city's skyline. And, like most Arab cities, it is a noisy place—honking autos, blaring radios, rattling trolleys, and people shouting, simply from the habit of making themselves heard.

The veil for women has largely disappeared from Syria—long ago in the villages and on the farms where it was simply impractical. In the city many of the modern women would find it archaic, though they do frequently substitute dark sunglasses, but these are ubiquitous in the Middle East for men, also.

Syrian businessmen and their wives—almost everyone in the relatively well-to-do class—have long ago adopted Western clothes, from the jacket and tie for men to the cocktail dresses of the younger women who gather in the numerous social and athletic clubs. There is, however, still a separation of men and women, both in the home when visitors come and down to separate sections of public parks and to special movie matinees for women only. In the villages the dress for men is the nightshirt-like *gallabia* over white cotton pants, and the long, baggy (usually red and ruffled) pants for women, worn under as many skirts as possible. The *gallabia* is also worn by many working-class city dwellers.

The people of Syria are predominately Arab and Semitic. They speak Arabic (and French) and worship in the Muslim faith. Perhaps 10 percent of the population is

Christian, several varieties of both Catholic and Protestant. Some 60,000 of these are Armenians who escaped the Turkish persecution of World War I and the years following.

Winters in Syria can be cold, sometimes with snow in the higher portions. Spring is lovely—and brief. Summer is hot—and long. From May to November the temperatures may be in the 100-degree range or higher, and Syrians are addicted to the siesta and avoiding the noonday sun. Business in the cities simply ceases, normally, from one to four in the afternoon.

TURKEY

Until 1925, Turkey remained a medieval state. The first quarter of the twentieth century had gone by before this country—which lies in both Europe and Asia, and which sits astride the Dardanelles, the Sea of Mamara, and the Bosporus and for four hundred years was the seat of the Ottoman Empire—recognized the modern world. The Turks had missed the Renaissance and the Industrial Revolution. Successive sultans in the fading days of the Empire had almost totally ignored the emerging sciences, customs, and thought of the times.

Modern Turkey began with the man, Mustafa Kemal Ataturk, born to Ali Riza the tax collector and his wife Zubeyde, in the poverty-marked Turkish quarter of the city of Salonika. That was the year 1881.

He was born just plain Mustafa. While in military school and still in his teens, an amused mathematics teacher added the "Kemal," meaning "perfection," because of the boy's passion always to be right. And, many years later, he became Mustafa Ataturk, literally "Mustafa, Father of the Turks."

Mustafa and his parents were Macedonians in that confused world of the turn of the century when the nations of Europe were playing a deadly game of check and checkmate with Czarist Russia, and each other, for the Balkan and the Middle Eastern pieces of the Ottoman Empire, which had become known by that time as the "Sick Man of Europe."

Mustafa Kemal completed military school and entered the army where his rapid rise in rank was almost miraculous, considering the fact that he was constantly preaching, organizing, and fomenting sedition. He participated in the revolt of the "Young Turks" (which gave rise to that phrase, still in popular use), fought brilliantly in the successful defense of Gallipoli, and on various other fronts in World War I.

After the war, while the Allies were busy setting up the complete dismemberment of the Ottoman Empire, Mustafa Kemal organized a revolt against both the Empire's Sultan and the Allies, formed a nationalist government in Ankara, drove invading Greeks off the Anatolian Plateau, and gained enough respect that the Italians and French withdrew from areas that had been assigned them without coercion. In 1922 the Allies agreed to an armistice and to granting the nationalists the territory which had originally been Turkey. In 1923, Mustafa Kemal became President of the first Republic of Turkey.

He had always been proud, ambitious, self-confident to the point of arrogance, successful, and an eminently capable man. Now, although he was ostensibly heading a democracy, Kemal was, in fact, exactly as much or as little the dictator as he wished to be. He had always wanted power and now he had it. He possessed Turkey, literally.

But unlike most monocrats, the way he preferred to use his power was for the good of his people.

The first changes Mustafa Kemal made were political. A parliament was elected and organized to be the repository of governmental power, although the President was the executive and chose his own cabinet.

He abolished the Ministry of Religious Affairs, banned old-time Muslim orders, took over religious property in the name of the state, and forbade religious instruction in the schools. He replaced Muslim holy law with European codes, took Turkish women out from behind their veils, abolished the *fez* in favor of the hat, and replaced the Arabic alphabet with the Latin form. In due course, Islam was disestablished for all official purposes and Turkey became a secular state. He promoted industry in an attempt to raise the national income and the standard of living. The effort was moderately successful. He established friendly relations with as many foreign nations as possible and, after first shunning foreign aid and investment, eventually accepted British economic assistance.

Mustafa Kemal Ataturk died in November of 1938, after four terms as President, and was succeeded by Ismet Inonu. He followed closely in Kemal's footsteps and led his country on a neutral tightrope walk through World War II. Turkey became an organizing member of the United Nations and joined NATO in 1952. The Turkish political system has gone through several changes since Inonu and today has both a President and Prime Minister, operating under a traditional parliamentary system.

The topography, people, and early history of Turkey are described in Chapters VII, VIII, and IX. The economy of today actually is based, as it always has been, on agriculture, and the growth has been greatly expanded in the past two decades. The main crops are cotton, tobacco, and grain.

Turkey is one of seven countries in the world permitted to export opium and is the second largest behind India. Legally the crop fills the world's legitimate requirement for opium-based drugs—mostly morphine and codeine—and comes from the opium-poppy cultivation which has existed in Turkey for centuries and is the livelihood for thousands of rural Turks living in the western Anatolian Plateau. In addition to the opium gum, the by-product seeds and stalks are also important for use as flavoring, fuel, and fodder.

In past years a sizeable portion of the opium crop always has been diverted for illegal reduction to heroin, providing most of the American supply, and in 1973 the United States paid Turkey compensation to ban the production. This was in effect for one year and then dropped, however. Both countries now carry out an intense cooperative campaign to control the illegal diversion.

CHAPTER XII

Lower Arabia

OMAN

PEOPLE'S DEMOCRATIC
REPUBLIC OF YEMEN

YEMEN ARAB REPUBLIC

OMAN

THE ancient land of Oman is one of several tenants of the Musandam Peninsula which thrusts like a spearhead into the Persian Gulf, separating it from the Gulf of Oman and the farther-along Indian Ocean. The other tenants are the United Arab Emirates.

Oman is a country of two parts, and one of those occupies the possibly strategic tip of the Peninsula, perhaps a thousand miles of aridity which pushes its nose boldly into the Straits of Hormus and to within fifty miles or so of Iran. Through this strait, in an endless stream of oversized tankers, passes two-thirds of all the oil in the world.

Oman itself is not a major oil producer, but it does collect in the neighborhood of $1.25 billion each year in oil revenues, sufficient to dwarf its former gross national income considerably.

The rest of Oman (the overall nation is about the size of Kansas) is separated from the Peninsula by some fifty miles of the United Emirates and stretches into a thousand-mile coastline, facing the Gulf of Oman on the northeast and the Arabian Sea on the south. It has one border with South Yemen and another with Saudi Arabia, where Omani territory tails off into the lifeless desert of the Empty Quarter. Neither of the boundaries is well-defined and this fact causes minor border troubles from time to time.

Most of Oman's 750,000 people live on a narrow strip along the Gulf of Oman known as the Al Batinah, a coastal plain which is fertile and receives enough rainfall to produce mostly dates but some bananas, mangoes, onions, wheat, coconuts, and tobacco. Only 0.2 percent of Oman's land is arable. The temperatures are high and so is the humidity. Rainfall fluctuates widely but averages only around three inches a year. The capital city of Muscat is on the Al Batinah coast and has a population of seven thousand persons.

Oman's ancient history is probably more interesting than its recent. Sumerian tablets three thousand years old mentioned it as the Land of Magan and chronicled its trade with ancient Sumerian cities, like Eridu and the Biblical Ur of the Chaldees. Far in the south the province of Dhofar produced tons of frankincense, the precious resin of an Arabic tree which was much used as an incense for religious ceremonies, and which probably found its way to neighboring Sheba for transshipment by its famous queen. The Roman naturalist Pliny the Elder knew of the island of Masirah, off Oman's east coast, identifying it as the Island of Turtles.

In more modern times the country was known as Muscat and Oman; it was converted to Islam during the era of Muhammad and had no contact with the West until 1508 when the Portuguese conquered the coastal region and gave strong signs of establishing permanent hegemony. The Sultan of Oman tossed them out in 1650, however, and except for a short period of Persian rule the land has been independent ever since.

The present ruling family of Said has been in power since the middle of the eighteenth century. The Sultan of Oman (the name of the country was changed officially to just Oman in 1970) is an absolute monarch who rules with the help of his ministers who are also mostly members of his family. There is no constitution or legislature, and no political parties. The judicial system in the more populous area is based on the Koran. Among the Bedouin and other desert dwellers, tribal law remains.

Foreign businessmen are welcome in Oman but the government discourages tourists and, indeed, there are few accommodations for them. Medical facilities are limited. Liquor is prohibited. The U.S. State Department advises feminine visitors against wearing shorts, short skirts, or sleeveless dresses.

PEOPLE'S DEMOCRATIC
REPUBLIC OF YEMEN

THE People's Democratic Republic of Yemen, more commonly known as South Yemen, has had a checkered career since about 1200 B.C. when it was part of several early kingdoms (Minaean, Sabaean, and Himyarite), was then conquered by the Christian Ethiopians, then by the Persians, and eventually, of course, by the Arab warriors of Islam.

It is still enjoying a turgid political life with close bonds to both Russia (from whom it gets military aid) and Red China, and a close alignment with several radical *fedayeen* groups of the Middle East, particularly the Popular Front for the Liberation of Palestine (PFLP). It claims ties with its sister state of North Yemen (Yeman Arab Republic) which is not quite sure how really close it wants those ties to be. It has never been recognized as a nation by its large neighbor, Saudi Arabia, with whom it has quarrelled occasionally, and it broke diplomatic ties with the United States in 1967, expelling the U.S. mission.

South Yemen's modern history, of course, is wrapped around the city and port of Aden, on the Gulf of Aden which leads to the Indian Ocean. By the 1830s the British

178

already had dreams of the Suez Canal and in addition needed a port in the vicinity of Aden to refuel its new steamships. Unable to get Aden by negotiation, Britain captured it in 1839, indemnified the ruling Sultan and raised the Union Jack. Thus Aden became part of the British Empire.

Its importance enhanced by the opening of the Suez Canal in 1869, South Yemen remained a colonial possession until 1961 when it was made a protectorate, and finally gained full independence in 1967, with intermittent financial and political troubles since. The country is presently governed by a three-man Presidential Council and a Council of Ministers. The chairman of the Presidential Council is also Chief of State. The Prime Minister is head of government. Power stems from the National Front (NF) Party, with leadership shared between the pro-Russia and the pro-China factions.

South Yemen has an area of 112,000 square miles, equal to the size of Wisconsin and Michigan combined, and a total population of a million and a half. Eighty percent of the population lives in rural areas, but Aden, the capital with 225,000 people, dominates the economy of the country. The entire gross national product, however, is probably not much over $150 million, largely derived from refueling of seagoing vessels. Aden also has an oil refinery and some small industry.

The coastline of South Yemen stretches for six hundred miles from the Gulf of Aden to the Arabian Sea, rising to mountains only a few miles inland. The climate is very hot and rainfall averages about three inches a year. Those residents of South Yemen who do not live in Aden are farmers (sorghum, millet, wheat, cotton, and coffee) or nomads. Quat, a mildly narcotic plant is also fairly widely grown.

YEMEN ARAB REPUBLIC

THE Yemen Arab Republic is part of an ancient land known as the Kingdom of Sheba, whose early history is obscure and only dimly known, but out of which did emerge one clear figure, romantic but very real, the Queen of Sheba.

It is true that her fame comes through her connection with another romantic figure of that time, Solomon, King of the Hebrews, but he had the advantage of being himself an historian; he had better access for inclusion in the records.

The time was around 950 B.C. The Kingdom of Sheba, like the Yemen of today, was located in the southwestern corner of the Arabian Peninsula, just north of the passage between the Red Sea and the Gulf of Aden.

Inland, separated from the Red Sea coast by the Tihama, a hot, desert-like strip forty miles wide, is a rather mountainous interior, terraced and well-watered for productive agriculture. It probably has been always thus, and because of its abundance of food, the Red Sea ports of ancient Sheba became important trading cities with the Far East.

Solomon, son of David, was a man of many dimensions. Reputedly he had seven hundred wives and three hundred

concubines. He married judiciously, and obviously cease-
lessly, the daughters of emperors, pharaohs, kings, all of
the nearby powers, in the age-old effort to cement good
relations with the neighbors. (Obviously, also, he must
have married at least some other ladies simply because
they attracted him.)

He also had, at this time, just completed two extraor-
dinary edifices in Jerusalem, one for Jehovah and another
for himself, the description of which take up four chapters
in the second book of Chronicles, and had established a
court so grand and so opulent that its reputation had trav-
eled far and wide. And this news, of course, reached Sheba
and the Queen.

The Queen of Sheba had her share of curiosity, but she
also had an excess of trading goods: her own frankincense
and myrrh, plus spices and jewelry of the Far East for
which she needed a market. King Solomon, she knew, had
his own ports on the Mediterranean and access to a wide
trading area. So, sending couriers ahead to announce her
arrival, she loaded a camel train with gifts and merchandise, and rode out across the Arabian desert to the Court
of King Solomon.

Both II Chronicles and I Kings in the Old Testament
make much of the visit—the Queen's awe at the grandeur
of the court, the food, the table settings, the servants and
their livery, the accoutrements of the King's guards. And
Solomon in turn made much of his visitor's beauty and
elegance, and her gifts. One line in the Song of Solomon
might have been written by or for her: "I am black but I
am comely, oh ye daughters of Jerusalem" and many

Biblical scholars believe that chapter 10, verse 13 of
I Kings should be interpreted that, among other presents,
Solomon gave her a child. (Menelik II, who created the
modern nation of Ethiopia in the early part of this cen-
tury, claimed to be a descendant of an earlier legendary
Menelik, son of Sheba and Solomon.)

The Yemen Arab Republic (also known as North
Yemen) of today has little of the glory of that past. The
country has an area of some 75,000 square miles (about
the size of Nebraska) and a population estimated at six
to seven million people, most of whom are Arabs; mostly,
also, they are former nomads, now settled in small villages
with surrounding farms, growing wheat, sorghum, cotton,
fruits, cattle, and sheep. Ancient Sheba, with a far smaller
population, was self-subsistent; so, too, was the North
Yemen of a generation or two ago. But disputes with
neighboring Saudi Arabia and civil wars, plus an extended
drought, have so weakened the country's productive capacity that today it depends on foreign aid, plus remit-
tances from Yemenis working abroad to support itself.
More than a million Yemenis work in Saudi Arabia alone,
mostly in the oil fields.

North Yemen has two climates: the coastal, which is hot
and dry, and the inland area, which has mountains up to
twelve thousand feet and often gets as much as thirty-five
inches of rainfall a year. Rivers, which flow the year
around inland, do not get across the forty-mile Tihama
stretch of desert to the coast.

Sana in the north central section, and over seven thousand feet high, is the capital and principal city. Taiz,

nearer the coast and in the south, is second in size. Hodeida, at the center of the Red Sea coast, is the largest port.

Sana has an airport and receives flights from Jidda, Cairo, and Asmara. All three of the major cities have reasonably adequate hotels. There are no railroads, but taxis can be rented by the trip or the day. Main roads are paved.

The United States had strained relations with North Yemen for a number of years but these were mended in 1972 and a full embassy established. Also an AID and a Peace Corps program.

CHAPTER **XIII**

Egypt and the Sudan

EGYPT

THE SUDAN

EGYPT

Alexander the Great, son of Philip of Macedonia, had conquered the only world he knew about by the time he had reached the mouth of the Nile in the year 332 B.C.

He may or may not have wept over the lack of further worlds to conquer (historians disagree), but he did pause there in Egypt, which had welcomed rather than resented his armed intrusion, and he paused at the mouth of the Nile to build a city to which he gave his name. Eleven years later Alexander, greatest of all the Greek generals, died of the fever at the age of thirty-three, but the city of Alexandria has lived on for more than two thousand years. Half of that time it was the capital of all Egypt.

It was also for centuries the largest city in the Western world, a great Mediterranean port and the center of both Greek and Hebrew culture. It was famous for its museum, probably the greatest in the world at that time, well before the birth of Christ, and an immense library which contained more than 900,000 scrolls written on the Egyptian marshland papyrus. The library was burned during the first Roman invasion when Caesar conquered both the country and its beautiful ruler, Cleopatra.

Alexandria became part of the Roman Empire, along

with the rest of Egypt in A.D. 30. She suffered under the Persians for a time and then, in 624, fell to the Arabs of Islam, who were sweeping over the area like a burning wind. They moved the capital to Cairo, where it has been since, but Alexandria remains historically one of the world's most romantic of cities and certainly one of its loveliest.

Egypt was almost constantly under foreign rule from the time of the Romans until the middle of this century. The Turks took over from the Arabs and the governments ranged from Ottoman to semiautonomous. Napoleon was in and out for a while. The final outsiders were the British. They moved in, in 1882, with the clear understanding that the occupation would be only temporary. They finally left, step by foot-dragging step three quarters of a century later, the last British trooper stepping off the sands of the Alexandrian shore in June, 1956.

Before the British, the French had obtained a ninety-nine-year concession to build and maintain a canal which would provide a waterway between the Mediterranean and the Red Sea. They organized the Suez Canal Company, and with European capital built the famous waterway, a ten-year project which was completed in 1869. The British bought up enough shares a few years later to share control with the French.

Egypt's advent into the world of modern affairs began with Gamal Abdel Nasser. (For the country's ancient history see Chapter VI and for its wars with Israel, Chapter III.) King Farouk had assumed the Egyptian throne in 1937 at the age of seventeen. He was handsome, exceedingly popular nationally, and during the first few years of his reign appeared to be the one man in the world of Arab leadership who might pull it together. He failed, however, to cope with either the internal politics of his own country or his own lighter inclinations, and on July 23, 1952, a young group of army officers seized power and established a nine-man Revolutionary Command Council to rule the country.

Farouk abdicated and went into exile (in Paris) with half a shipload of personal possessions, and, after two years of political infighting, Nasser emerged as chairman of the Command Council and Prime Minister. Under Nasser, Egypt did begin to move toward leadership in the spheres of Islamic, African, and Arab affairs. Nasser flirted politically with both the East and the West, built the Aswan Dam which greatly increased the arable land in the Nile basin, nationalized the Suez Canal, and engaged in a couple of ill-advised wars with the Israelis.

His death on September 28, 1970, seemed almost a national calamity, but his place was taken smoothly by his Vice-President, Anwar Sadat, who had been a long-time associate and close friend. Sadat was inclined to move his government's policies more toward the West, including a reestablishment of friendly relations with the United States.

The Arab Republic of Egypt, its official name today, leads the Arab world in size, population, industry, and armed forces. The Egyptians are foremost in arts and literature, publishing and film making. They also are preeminent in another culture and exercise form which has been well exported to the West, particularly to the United States—belly dancing.

Half of Egypt's total labor force of ten million is engaged in agriculture, the basis of the nation's economy. (One of Nasser's betterment moves was to create an effective land reform program, breaking up huge estates and redistributing land to rural families. No family may now own more than one hundred acres.) Industry, largely centered in Cairo, accounts for 20 percent of the gross national product and about 35 percent of the total exports. There is a little oil offcoast and in the Western Desert. (The Israelis took over the desert oil as a prize of war for several years.)

The capital city of Cairo is the largest in the Middle East with three and a half million people. Alexandria has two and a half. The vast majority of Egyptians are about the same as they were when the pyramids were built, basically of Hamitic origin (Ham was the son of Noah, after whom the Hamitic languages were named, a word meaning "swarthy" in Hebrew), and they cling to their centuries-old ancestry and culture. Among the minorities are three million Christian Copts, who have declined conversion to Islam for a millennium, fifty thousand nomadic Bedouins, and a handful of Nubians, some of them descended from the palace slaves of a few hundred years back.

THE SUDAN

THE Sudan is a land of sixteen million people and more than one hundred languages. It has scores of diverse ethnic groups, regional cultures, customs, loyalties, and a split personality. The larger and more advanced north is Arabic and almost Egyptian. The smaller southern section is pure Africa. They are as different as orthodox Muslim and witchcraft.

The north had been under strong Egyptian influence since the time of Tuthmosis I who ruled Egypt about 1525 B.C., along with the north two-thirds of the Sudan, then called Cush. Later (around 700 B.C.) the Cushites formed their own dynasty, took over Egypt for a while and, after retiring before the invading Assyrians, continued a Sudanese empire which lasted a thousand years with the capital at Meroe, today the site of a lost civilization waiting for someone to dig into it.

The Sudan is the largest country in Africa. It lies across the middle reaches of the Nile and is bounded by eight countries and the Red Sea. The countries are, clockwise from midnight; Egypt, Ethiopia, Kenya, Uganda, Zaire, the Central African Republic, Chad, and Libya. The Red Sea lies between the Egyptian and the Ethiopian borders.

In the far south, Sudan has tropical rain forests and

savannas, those tropical grasslands dotted with occasional trees, singly or in small clumps. Moving northward, there are vast swamplands, then open and semitropical savannas mixed with scrublands. Near the Red Sea and northern areas are the arid, sandy hills of the Nubian Desert. Near the center of the nation is the Gezira area which lies between the Blue and White Nile before they meet at Khartoum. This area, like Egypt, depends on the flood waters of the rivers to irrigate the soil for productive crops. Many parts of the south have sufficient rainfall for agriculture.

The climate is varied also. It is hot and humid in the south. The temperature along the coast is tempered by the breezes from the Red Sea. The central area (including Khartoum) has a desert climate, averaging about 100 degrees F. for ten months a year and then cooling off to around 94 degrees in January and February. The humidity is very low, however, and the weather moderates after sunset.

Sudan's three principal cities, Khartoum, Omdurman, and Khartoum North, form a single metropolitan area where the Blue and White Nile join, and have a combined population of about 700,000, although there are some two million people in the general area of the Gezira.

The more modern political life of the Sudan has been extremely varied. It was Christianized for a while, then fell under the influence of the Muslims and eventually became a collection of small states until it was unified again by Egypt in 1821. Sixty years later Muhammad Ahmed, a messianic figure who called himself the Mahdi, or Leader of the Faithful, led a successful revolution.

By this time Britain had already taken a not-too-willing Egypt under her wing and, moved further by the spirit of colonization (though also horrified by the stories of government-sponsored and utterly ruthless slave trading), both prodded and aided Egypt into action.

British General Charles Gordon—who was better known as "Chinese Gordon" for his military exploits in China—was sent in to subdue the Mahdi. Instead, his forces were hemmed in at Khartoum, besieged, and Gordon himself killed. This was in 1885.

Four years later Horatio Herbert Kitchener led another Anglo-Egyptian force into Sudan, met and crushed the Mahdi's followers at Omdurman. Kitchener's later career included becoming Britain's Secretary for War in World War I, but when he was elevated to a high title, he chose to be known as Lord Kitchener of Khartoum.

Sudan remained under British and Egyptian domination until 1953 when all parties signed an agreement providing for self-government, and Sudan finally became wholly independent in 1956. The country has one party, the Sudanese Socialist Union, which is supported by the military. Most of the leadership is supplied by the Arabic north.

Political life in the Democratic Republic of the Sudan continues to be eventful. There have been economic difficulties, military coups, strikes, riots, and mutinies. The latest revolt in far south Equatoria Province resulted, after seventeen years of strife, into virtual autonomy for the entire southern region on all internal matters. The central government in Khartoum has an elected assembly and President, who is also the Prime Minister.

The Sudan's gross national product is just under $2 billion, derived mostly from cotton, cotton seed, peanuts, gum arabic, and sesame seed. There is some light industry and a modest reserve of metals, but no oil as yet.

CHAPTER **XIV**

North Africa

ALGERIA

LIBYA

MOROCCO

TUNISIA

ALGERIA

THE French government of Charles X, looking for a political diversion which might please his people, in 1830 wrested Algeria from centuries of Turkish domination, and annexed it in 1842. The French then exploited it for a century and only gave it up in 1962, after eight years of bitter guerrilla warfare and terrorism in both countries.

Algeria really belonged, and always has, to the Berbers who have comprised the majority population of this part of Africa for as many years as history records. Between then and very recent times, they have been ruled by a succession of invaders attracted by the fertile six hundred miles of Mediterranean coastline—Carthaginians, Romans, Arabs, Ottoman Turks, and finally, the French. In parts of the seventeenth and eighteenth centuries the country's major resource was piracy.

Today the Democratic and Popular Republic of Algeria, as the country is officially known, has a remarkably stable government which professes a policy of independence and nonalignment. She vehemently supports the Third World viewpoint in international affairs and has been actively involved in the Organization of the Non-Aligned States. She has a strong affinity for such "liberation" movements that she considers to be legitimate, and is a vocal and probably financial supporter of the Palestine Liberation Organization and the southern African nationalistic groups.

Algeria broke off diplomatic relations with the United States in 1967 over the Egyptian-Israeli war, but they were resumed in 1974 after a period of gradual improvement during which the U.S. Secretary of State visited Algeria and Algerian President Houari Boumediene paid a call to Washington.

Algeria is a large country, a million square miles (about one-third as large as the United States), and has a population of more than sixteen million people, nearly all of them Muslims of Berber, Arab, or Berber-Arab mixed stock. There is a total European population of about 75,000. The country lies between Morocco and Tunisia, bordering also on Libya, Niger, Mali, Mauritania, and the Spanish Sahara. Two ranges of the Atlas Mountains cross the country laterally and divide it into three zones: the Tell (Arabic for "hill"), the narrow fertile coastal plain along the Mediterranean with a moderate climate and generous rainfall; the High Plateau region stretching from the Tell to the Saharan Atlas, averaging three thousand feet in altitude, mostly rocky plains and desert with a limited rainfall; and the third and largest region by far in the south which is simply the Sahara Desert, devoid of vegetation except for a little scrubby pasture and a few oases.

The capital and largest city, with about one million people, is Algiers. Also on the coast are Oran and Annaba, while Constantine lies a few miles inland.

The Algerian economy today is almost totally government-controlled, including economic planning, development, and administration. Government agencies control most of foreign trade, all major industries, most of the distribution and retail systems, all public utilities, and the nation's banking and credit system. In the decade after independence, Algeria nationalized all major foreign business interests and many private Algerian companies as well, all compensated for, usually satisfactorily.

Algerian farmers raise wheat, barley, oats, grapes, citrus fruits, olives, dates, vegetables, and tobacco, and there is some industry, including wine making and textile, but the country's major resources are, of course, petroleum and petroleum-related products.

Production of crude oil began in the mid-Sahara in 1958 at Hassi Massaoud and over near the Libyan frontier. By 1966 fields had opened in a dozen locations and by 1970 gross domestic production grew at an average annual rate of 11.2 percent up to a daily production of more than a million barrels a day and an average return to the government—after the price rises of 1973—of about $4 billion. There is a state oil monopoly, SONATRACH, which has joint-venture agreements with five American oil companies.

Equally important with the oil itself is the fact that Algeria has the world's fourth largest natural gas reserve and is devoting a large share of oil income to the development of these deposits for export in both liquefied form and to promote local industry.

Algeria has plowed back a fair share of her oil income

into infrastructure. She now has almost 50,000 miles of highways, and 2,500 miles of railways, and three international airports with ten smaller supporting ports. She also has her own state-owned air line. And, most modern in a modern world, Algeria is one of the first countries in the world to adopt an earth satellite telecommunications system to serve her telephone system, telex, and television networks.

LIBYA

LIFE arrived for Libya in 1958 when the first important oil strikes were made. Ten years later Libya was the fourth largest oil exporter in the world and by the latter 1970s this arid little North African land was taking in so many billions of petrodollars she was unable to spend them.

The Libyan Arab Republic lies on the north central coast of Africa. Just west are Algeria and Tunisia whose history Libya virtually duplicates; that is, she had the same invaders, the same despoilers and oppressors but, unlike in Algeria and Tunisia, they left only a few scattered ruins as evidence of ancient cities—Sabratha, Leptis, and Magna. There are no traces of these ancient cultures or people.

More than 90 percent of Libya's terrain is desert, or almost-desert—barren, desolate, rock-strewn plains and miles of rolling seas of sand, with two unimportant ranges of low mountains in the northeast and northwest. There are no rivers in all of Libya which run the year around. It rains, usually, every three years, irregularly and scantily. The temperature is usually high, often affected by the *ghibli*, a hot, dry wind from the south, laden with dust. It may last one day or four in the spring or fall and it can raise the temperature as much as forty degrees in just an hour or so.

Only 7 percent of the land, along the coast and on a few oases and hillsides, is arable. The total population of just over two million would average 3.2 persons per square mile if scattered about. Tripoli, the capital with 250,000 people, and Benghazi, are the two important cities.

Italy invaded Libya and made it her colony in 1911, taking it away from the Ottoman Turks. The British and French divided it up after World War II, but only temporarily. King Idris went to a newly formed United Nations and, in 1951, Libya became the first country to gain independence through the action of that organization. After years of political unrest, a group of young army officers led by Colonel Muammar al-Gaddafi, overthrew the monarchy and established rule by Revolutionary Command Council, the usual thing in Middle East coups. The revolt was remarkable for the accompanying events which did not occur: there was no opposition, no fighting, no arrests, no executions. Aged King Idris I went quietly off to exile in Egypt.

The policy of the new regime became very much what it professed to be—one of Arab nationalism. The last British military left in 1970 and the Americans, long nesting on Wheelus Air Force Base under a wartime lease, moved out a little later the same year. Enforcement of a law which had been on the books for years requiring that all businesses operating in Libya be under Libyan control was effected, and many were sequestered, with payment usually made in government bonds. In 1969 there were more than twenty oil companies operating in Libya. All have been nationalized, some completely, some in part. The Libyan government took the lead in the 1973 price battle with the oil giants and since then has deliberately held down production—partly to keep the price up, but mostly to conserve her reserves.

Shortly after the 1969 coup, a Provisional Constitution was drawn up which established the twelve-man Revolutionary Command Council as the country's highest authority. It "exercises the functions of supreme sovereignty and legislation and decides the general policy of the State on behalf of the people." The RCC controls the military and has the power to declare war, make treaties, and name the Prime Minister and Cabinet. The Chairman of the RCC is in effect the head of state.

Under Colonel Gaddafi the new regime launched, along with the program of Arab nationalism, a cultural program which was peculiar to Libya. All European and American executives, teachers, technicians, and doctors were replaced by Arabs. Only Arabic was permitted on street signs, official stationery, and publications. Foreign passports had to be in Arabic, too, and the prohibition on alcoholic drinks was revived. There was a return to some of the laws of the Koran. One was the amputation of the hands of thieves.

Under its policy of Arab nationalism, the Libyan government quite naturally supports strongly Muslim causes throughout the world, strongly opposes the existence of Israel—to the point of resisting peaceful settlement of the Arab-Israel problem—and strongly advocates the elimination of any large foreign power influence in the Middle East, either American or Soviet.

MOROCCO

Morocco has always been the setting for dreams. Here, on an island a little offshore, Hercules stole the golden apples of the Hesperides nymphs as one of his twelve improbable labors; here the Casbah is the temptress of adventuring love, and Casablanca is romantic at any age.

With coastlines on both the Atlantic Ocean and the Mediterranean Sea, and separated from the continent of Europe by only a few miles of the Strait of Gibraltar, Morocco has had an unusual upbringing. In very early days both the Phoenicians and then the Carthaginians established outposts on her coasts for trading. The Romans, a little later, turned northern Morocco into their own province of Mauritania Tingitana, pushing the inland borders south of Rabat and Fez. The faithful of Islam raided the Moroccan lands in the seventh century, and a hundred years later Idris, a descendant of the Prophet Muhammad through his daughter Fatima, established a dynasty there with the help of the Berber tribesmen.

In the eleventh century a sect of warrior monks, the Almoravides from the south, took over the entire country and moved into Spain where they battled the Christians—including one of Spain's most famous heroes, Rodrigo

Diaz de Vivar, known to history, song, and drama as El Cid.

Morocco fell into France's "sphere of influence" early in the twentieth century, when France and England were dividing up the world of the Middle East (although Spain didn't entirely relinquish its claim to some authority). In 1912 it became a protectorate of both these European nations and, finally, after World War II and several revolts, gained full independence in 1956.

Present-day Moroccans, the descendants of aboriginal North African Berbers and Arabs, make up most of the sixteen million people in the country. There are also some 115,000 Europeans, mostly French and Spanish, and about 30,000 Muslim Jews. The principal language is Arabic although there, as in most parts of North Africa, it is safer to speak in French because of the wide difference in dialects.

Morocco is an eminently civilized country and a center of learning for North Africa. The largest university, Muhammad V, in Rabat, has ten thousand students, studying medicine, law, the sciences, and liberal arts. Rabat also has the Muhammadia School of Engineers and the Hassan II Agromatic Institute. In the religious capital of Fez is the thousand-year-old Karouine University, which attracts Islamic students from around the world to study Islamic law and theology. The country has a literacy rate of 25 percent for men but only 7 percent for women.

Although Western attire predominates among the men of Morocco and has been adopted by many women there, the native dress is still prevalent and the most colorful of any Middle Eastern country. Most common is the *djellaba*, a long, hooded robe (usually a deep blue in the south) much like the habit of the Franciscan monks, and native footwear is the *babouche*, an open-heeled slipper with long pointed toes which frequently curl upward. Berber women go unveiled in their native villages but will cover their faces when going outside. At parties and other social functions, Moroccan women wear the lovely, colorful *kaftans*, usually with intricately designed gold belts.

Topographically, Morocco is divided between the open, fertile plains of the northwest and the economically poor mountain and plateau areas of the eastern and south sections. The Atlantic coastal plains are by far the most densely populated. The economy of Morocco depends heavily on agriculture with almost 70 percent of the people using it as a source of direct or indirect living. The agricultural methods are primitive. The wooden plow, hoe, and pointed stick are still much in use by the Moroccan peasant, mostly because the tiny plots of land division make any kind of modern farming impractical.

Rabat is the capital of Morocco, although Casablanca is by far the largest city with some two million people. Tangier, sitting just across the straits from Gibraltar is the easiest for tourists to visit. Fez and Meknes are northern inland cities and Marrakech dominates the south.

The King of Morocco has, since independence, exercised strong political and religious control over the people, but a new constitution presented by King Hassan II in 1972 and approved by referendum makes the government more responsive to popular will. There is a unicameral parliament with increased powers, elected for four-year terms. The King names, and may dismiss, the Prime Minister and cabinet members. Members of the Supreme Court are also appointed by the King.

King Hassan II, who succeeded his father, Muhammad V, in 1961, has not had the smoothest of reigns. There were civil rights riots in 1965 and attempted coups in both 1971 and 1972, with later executions. And in 1975 came the problem concerning the Spanish Sahara, the arid little country on Morocco's southwestern border, separating it from Mauritania.

Spain relinquished her claim to the Spanish Sahara as an overseas territory in the Madrid Accord of November 14, 1975, and both Morocco and Mauritania immediately asserted possession. A solution of sorts was reached in February, 1976, when a rump session of the Spanish Sahara Parliament met in the capital of El Aaiun and declared the northern two-thirds under Moroccan control and the southern one-third under Mauritania's. This became effective although it wasn't quite satisfactory to the United Nations and possibly not to the Saharans, either, and may be subject to change.

TUNISIA

Tunisia is about the size of the state of Georgia, lies wedged in between Algeria and Libya, has a thousand-mile coastline along the Mediterranean and a population of some six million people, most of them Arabs.

For a nation so small, Tunisia has led a very eventful life for her three thousand-odd years of recorded history. It begins with the establishment on the Bay of Tunis of the city of Carthage, in the ninth century before Christ, by Phoenician Queen Dido, the part legendary, part real-life lady who, it is told, threw herself on a blazing funeral pyre when her lover, Aeneas, sailed away and left her. Carthage, of course, went on in spite of that to a position of both Naval and commercial supremacy and is associated with many famous names of history, Hannibal among them.

Carthage was destroyed in the Second Punic War and then rebuilt by Augustus at the dawn of the Christian era, becoming second only to Rome in the Empire. Then came the Germanic Vandals, the regime of Byzantium, the Arabs of Islam, and the Ottoman Empire of Turkey.

And, of course, Tunisia was one of the belligerents of the Tripolitan War of 1801-1805 with the United States. Tunisia was then one of the Barbary States—Algeria, Tunisia, and Tripolitania (now western Libya). The war made a hero out of Stephen Decatur, who forced the Dey of Algeria to sign a treaty ending the payment of tribute to the Barbary pirates and who also originated the famous toast with lines ending "Our country . . . may she always be in the right; but our country right or wrong."

France took over the well-being of Tunisia in 1881, making the country a protectorate two years later. The Tunisians began making moves toward independence right after World War I, to which the French paid little attention until the emergence in 1934 of a new leader, Habib ben Ali Bourguiba. The Tunisians were content to negotiate for almost twenty years and then resorted to guerrilla warfare. The French finally granted independence in 1956 and the last French troops left two years later (though France still maintains a Naval base at Bizerte, by treaty). Bourguiba was elected President in 1957 and the country has enjoyed political stability since.

As a nonaligned nation, Tunisia maintains relations with both the West and the East, with a strong leaning Westward, particularly to the United States. The President determines national policy and his bills have priority before an elected assembly. He appoints the Prime Minister and cabinet.

Tunisia has three areas. The north is lightly wooded and fertile, the scene of most of the country's agricultural activity; the coastal plain provides grazing land for livestock and also is dotted with olive groves, and the southern region, bordering on and very much like the Sahara Desert. Agriculture is the backbone of the Tunisian economy, along with commercially exploitable deposits of phosphates, iron ore, lead, and zinc. Oil was discovered in 1964 and furnishes enough for domestic use and exports of about a quarter of a billion dollars worth annually.

The capital city of Tunis with its population of 800,000 bestrews itself around the lake of the same name near the site of ancient Carthage. Ships enter the lake through La Goulette, quite literally "a throat," from the Bay of Tunis and the Medierranean. La Goulette with its towering battlements on each shore was the first line of defense when Tunis was a pirate stronghold and herself eminently subject to invasion, and the lake—muddy-bottomed and shallow, treacherously narrow passaged—was the second.

Modern Tunis is a seething mixture of West and East— carts and taxis, beggars, vendors, horns, radios, auto fumes; it combines all the most unattractive elements of any Middle Eastern city. Old Tunis was designed long before machines had invaded civilization and has the charm one hopes to find in strange places. Its *souks* are not quiet but their stalls are crammed with every form of merchandise from every part of the world, its merchants have a dignified courtesy, and its winding streets, much too narrow for an automobile, give occasional glimpses through open doorways of charming gardens and fountains and an older, more placid manner of life.

Suggestions for Further Reading

For general reference and survey:

The Middle East and North Africa, 1975-76. Europa Publications Ltd., London. This annual work covers history, economics, government, politics, and statistics, generously and effectively.

Any of the more modern works of English author W. B. Fisher, whose contributions add greatly to the excellence of *The Middle East and North Africa* (above).

For a detailed picture of the Middle East oil situation:

Sampson, Anthony. *The Seven Sisters.* The Viking Press, New York, 1975.

For an interesting picture of the Middle East financial situation:

Field, Michael. *A Hundred Million Dollars a Day.* Praeger Publishers, Inc., 1976.

For an unbiased textbook approach (and mostly up to date), all recommended by the Middle East Studies Association of North America, Inc., after a survey of some eighty books used in secondary education:

Bucher, Henry, Jr., *The Third World: The Middle East.* Pendulum Press, West Haven, Conn., 1973.

Cambridge Press. *The Middle East: History, Culture, People.* New York, 1972.

Cleveland, Ray L. *The Middle East and South Asia.* Stryker-Post Publications, Washington, D.C., 1973.

Peretz, Don. *The Middle East. Selected Readings.* Houghton Mifflin Company, Boston, 1973.

Randall, John R. *Middle East.* Ginn and Company, Lexington, Mass., 1974.

Scholastic Book Services. *The Middle East.* New York, 1972.

Stavrianos, L. S. *A Global History of Man.* Allyn & Bacon, Boston, 1968.

Tachau, Frank. *The Middle East.* The Macmillan Company, New York, 1970.

For the military point of view:

Lewis, Jesse W. *The Strategic Balance in the Mediterranean.* Foreword by retired Admiral Elmo R. Zumwalt, Jr. The American Enterprise Institute for Public Policy Research, Washington, D.C., 1976.

For the Jewish point of view:

History, from 1880. From material originally published in the *Encyclopaedia Judaica.* Keter Publishing House, Ltd., Jerusalem, Israel, 1973.

For the Arab point of view:

Sharobi, Hisham. *Palestine and Israel: The Lethal Dilemma.* Pegasus, New York, 1969.

Turki, Faway. *The Disinherited.* Monthly Review Press, New York, 1972.

For the State Department point of view:

Background Notes. Department of State, Office of Media Service, Bureau of Public Affairs. (These are concise studies, mostly up to date, on each country, available at the Government Printing Office.)

For information and advice:

The Near East Section of the Library of Congress and the Middle East Institute Library, both in Washington, D.C.

Index

Abqaiq oil field, 136
Abraham, father of religions, 6
  in Palestine, 77
  journey into Canaan, 55
  wives and descendants, 77, 89, 90
Absalom, 56
Abu Dhabi, 26, 143, 144, 145
Aden, 178-180
Ahmed, Muhammad, 192, 193
Ajman, 143
Akkadians, 63, 90
Al Batinah, 176
Aleppo, 105, 165, 166
  famed souks of, 166
Alexander the Great, 72, 79, 187
  builds Alexandria, 187
Alexandria, 187
  center of olden culture, 187, 188
Algeria, 111, 197-200
  agriculture, 199
  geography and people, 198
  government, 197, 198
  independence from France, 197
  nationalization of industry, 199
  natural gas, 199
  relations with United States, 198
Algiers, 95, 198
Almoravides, 204
Amman, 158
  history, 159, 160
  modern city, 160
Amorites, 75
Ankara, 83, 101
Annaba, 198
Anti-Lebanon Mountains, 105
Aqaba, 31
Arab Information Center, 49
Arab Report, 49
Arab-Israeli wars, 26
  of Independence, 29
  of 1956, 31
  Six-Day War, 32
  Yom Kippur War, 33

Arabian Peninsula, 103, 107, 108
  climate, 108
  countries of, 108
  people, 108, 109
Arabs, 89, 90, 107, 108, 121, 126, 140,
  160, 167, 197, 203, 205
Aramco (Arabian American Oil
  Company), 136-138
Aref, 'Abd al-Salam Muhammad,
  130
Aref, General Abdal Rahman Mu-
  hammad, 130
Armenians, 101, 102, 126, 168
Asir, 140
Assyria, 107
Assyrians, 72, 76, 90, 106, 126
Aswan Dam, 67, 111, 189
Ataturk, Mustafa Kemal, 83, 91, 169
  early life, 170
  leader of rebellion, 170
  military record, 170
  rule of fifteen years, 171
Augustus, 72, 208
Aurelian, Emperor, 164
'Ayn, al-, 144, 145

Ba'ath Party, 130
Babylon, 53, 75, 131
Babylonians, 75, 76
Baghdad, ancient and modern city,
  95, 104, 106, 131, 132
  Baghdad Pact, 129
  divisions of Karkh and Rasafa,
  131
  meeting to organize OPEC, 15-17
Bahrain, 108, 115
  banking center, 116
  climate and history, 116, 117
  islands of, 115
  oil and industry, 116
  politics of, 117
  rulers, 117